Discovering
OLD BOARD GAMES

R. C. Bell

Shire Publications Ltd

CONTENTS

Introduction ...	...	...	...	...	...	...		3
Glossary ...	...	...	...	...	...	...		4
1. Race games	...	...	...	...	...	...		6
2. War games	...	...	...	...	...	...		21
3. Games of position	...	...	...	...	...			48
4. Mancala games	...	...	...	...	...			63
5. Calculation games	...	...	...	...	...			68
6. Dice games	...	...	...	...	...	...		73
Making boards and pieces ...	...	...	...	...				77
Bibliography	...	...	...	...	...	...		78
Index ...	...	...	...	...	...	...		79

ACKNOWLEDGEMENTS

The author wishes to acknowledge information and assistance given by correspondents in many parts of the world, including Mr K. Yano, Kobe, Japan; Miss E. Scott, H.M. Consul, Stuttgart, Germany; Lars Berglund, Hagersten, Sweden; Dr R. Pankhurst, Addis Ababa, Ethiopia; Miss A. M. D. Ashley, Salisbury, England; Mr K. R. Dunn, Long Beach, California, U.S.A.; and Mr J. Mosesson, Stowmarket, England.

The author has also been helped in translating foreign articles by Mr M. C. Oswald, Newcastle-upon-Tyne, (German); Miss Fiona Brookes, Durham, (French); Mr J. Mosesson, Stowmarket, (Swedish); and Mr K. Yano, Kobe, (Japanese).

The author and publishers wish to thank the Oxford University Press for allowing material previously published in *Board and Table Games of Many Civilisations, Vols I and II*, to be included in this present work.

The author is indebted to the curator of the Brunei National Museum for obtaining an article written in Malay on pasang; and to Mr Rashid of the Department of Physiology, Singapore University, for translating it into English.

Printed in Great Britain by Hunt Barnard Printing Ltd, Aylesbury, Bucks.

INTRODUCTION

Interest in old board games may arise from finding some bygone relic in an antique shop, seeing a display on the shelves of a museum, from stumbling across obscure games in travellers' accounts, or in archaeological references to fragmentary gaming-equipment discovered on ancient sites.

This book has been written to provide the enquirer with some of the answers to questions he may wish to ask, and to whet his curiosity to explore deeper into the curious byways of man's progress as revealed by a study of his leisure diversions.

Board games fall conveniently into six groups: Race games—with the object of reaching some part of the board with one or more pieces before the opponent. War games—in which the destruction of an opposing formation, the capture of a specific piece, or the occupation of an enemy citadel is achieved. Games of position—where the players strive to occupy particular squares or to marshal their pieces on defined portions of the board, or to occupy more area than their opponent. Mancala games—which depend upon the rapid calculation of the numbers of pieces in particular cups and form a distinct and widespread group of games. Calculation games—which were originally based on the philosophy of numbers developed by Pythagoras. Dice games—the throws of dice are interpreted in some competitive way.

Most games fall easily into one of these groups, but a few can be included with equal justification in either of two groups. In Tablan there is a dual objective of capturing enemy pieces and occupying enemy squares and it could be classified as a war game, though probably better as a game of position; while Conspiracy can be regarded as a race game with the devil taking the hindmost, or as a game of position with one player occupying one more shelter than the other.

For ease of reference the games have been arranged in rough chronological order within each group, the earlier games usually being simpler, and the most recent more elaborate.

Archaeologists tend to disregard the importance of games in indicating contacts between civilisations. A current archaeological problem concerns the connection, if any, in the Bronze Age between the Wessex Culture and Egypt. Faience beads have been recovered from graves in both areas, and this has been advanced by some as evidence of intercourse between the two societies. Chemical analysis of the glazes of the beads shows a far higher tin content in the British beads, but in spite of this some still argue that they were exported from Egypt. During this period of *c.* 1500 B.C. several games including Senat, played on thirty squares, Tau, the Palm Tree Game, and others were played in Egypt, and boards, pieces and dice are found frequently in burials there whereas no gaming equipment has ever been reported from the Long or Round Barrows of the Wiltshire plain. This is an indication, if one is needed, that there was minimal or no contact between these two civilisations, although we know that the Egyptians at this period possessed ships capable of making the voyage from the Nile to Britain without difficulty.

GLOSSARY

Column: See figure 1.

Crownhead: Spaces on which a piece becomes promoted to a king.

Custodian capture: Capture by trapping an opponent's piece between two of one's own.

Diagonal move: The piece moves diagonally.

Die: The singular of dice.

File: See figure 1.

Fork: A term used in chess when two of a player's pieces are simultaneously attacked by an enemy piece, and only one can be moved to safety at the next turn of play.

Huff: Removal of a piece which has infringed a rule.

Intervention: Capture by a piece occupying the point immediately between two enemy pieces, when the latter are removed from the board.

Ladder: The positioning of pieces to enable a piece to advance rapidly by a series of short leaps.

Long die: A four-sided die.

Long leap: A jump by a piece over another piece to land beyond, with vacant spaces intervening on either or both sides of the captured piece.

Open-ended fork: A term used in positional games, when a player is faced with the impossible task of blocking both ends of a line in a single turn of play.

Orthogonal move: The piece moves along a rank or file.

Point: The intersection of two lines.

Replacement: A capture made by a piece alighting on a space occupied by an enemy piece, the latter being moved from the board.

Rank: See figure 1.

Row: See figure 1.

Short leap: A capture made by a piece jumping over an enemy piece on an adjacent space, to land onto the space immediately beyond. (c.f. a long leap.)

4

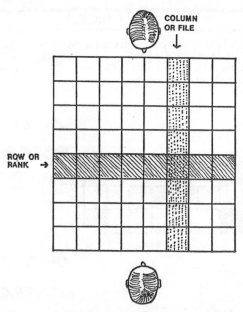

1. *Diagram to show column or file, and row or rank.*

1. RACE GAMES

The earliest known complete gaming boards were found in the Royal Tombs of Ur in Iraq by Sir Leonard Woolley, and these date from about 3000 B.C. (figure 2). They were all of one type though varying in the skill of their construction and the richness of their materials.

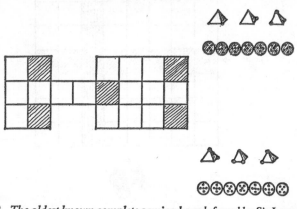

2. The oldest known complete gaming-board, found by Sir Leonard Woolley at Ur in the Royal Tombs, c. 3000 B.C. Note the pyramidal dice.

The simplest board consisted of little squares of shell, with red or blue centres, set in bitumen on the upper surface of a shallow box which contained seven black and seven white counters and six pyramidal dice, each with two of its four points tipped in colour. No rules survive, but the game appears to have been a race-track with the progress of the pieces controlled by scores indicated by throws of the dice. The significance of the marked squares on the board is unknown.

Senat

In 1922 Howard Carter opened the tomb of the ancient Egyptian king Tutankhamun who died in 1352 B.C. Among the treasures buried with him were four gaming boards, all of the same type, and similar in style to those from Ur made some fifteen hundred years earlier.

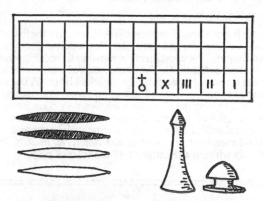

3. *An ancient Egyptian gaming-board, c. 1500 B.C., now in the British Museum. Typical gaming pieces are shown below at the right, and at the left gambling sticks similar to, though less elaborate than those found in the tomb of Tutankhamun.*

The largest and finest of the Egyptian boards was on display at the Tutankhamun exhibition in London in 1972. The box stood on an ebony stand in the form of a bed-frame with feline legs and paws which rested on guilded heels. Beneath the heels was an ebony sledge. The upper surface of the box was veneered with ebony and inlaid with thirty ivory squares, five being inscribed.

The under-surface of the box carried a second board of twenty squares, with three of the squares in the middle row being inscribed: one with the kneeling figure of Heh, the god of a million years; another with two thrones in pavilions, the sign for a jubilee festival; and the third with the hieroglyphic signs for life, stability and welfare. The pieces were missing, possibly having been made of precious metal and stolen by tomb-robbers in antiquity, but standard boards contained playing pieces of faience, five or seven for each player, one set being conical, and the other like little cotton-reels.

The rules of play are unknown, but it appears to have been a race game controlled by the throws of four casting sticks made of black ebony in the upper half and white ivory in the lower. One pair had the ends shaped into the form of a human finger-nail, and the other the head of a fox.

The board with the thirty squares was used for the game of Senat.

7

Ludus Duodecim Scriptorum

Boards for this favourite game of the Romans in the first century B.C. have been recovered from archaeological sites throughout the Roman Empire. The usual form consisted of three horizontal rows of twelve spaces (figure 4). The players moved their pieces according to the throws of three cubic dice marked '1' to '6', the score of any pair of opposing faces adding up to seven. Cheating was prevented by throwing the dice into a *fritillus*, a wooden tower about ten inches high with a spiral staircase inside. The dice fell down the staircase and spilled out onto the playing surface through a small exit. Ovid mentions the game in *Ars Amatoria, iii 363f*, but unfortunately without a description of the rules of play.

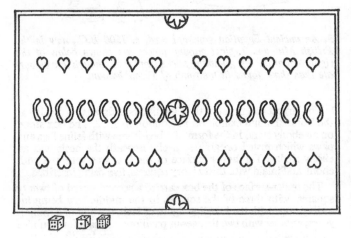

4. A Ludus Duodecim Scriptorum board from Denbighshire, now in the National Museum of Wales, c. A.D. 125.

Tabula

During the first century A.D. Ludus Duodecim Scriptorum was replaced in fashionable circles by Tabula, a variant with only two rows of spaces (figure 5). Agathias, a scholastic of Myrine in Asia (A.D. 527-67), described a disastrous game played by Emperor Zeno fifty years earlier, and this sixth-century record enabled the rules to be recovered.

8

Rules for Tabula

1. The game was played on a board of twenty-four spaces by two players, each having fifteeen pieces of his own colour.

2. The moves of the pieces were controlled by the alternate throws of three six-sided dice and the numbers exposed could be used to move one piece by the total throw, or two pieces by the score of one die and two dice respectively, or three pieces each by the score of one die. If a throw of 2: 4: 6: was made, one piece could move twelve spaces as long as each resting space was clear: i.e. 2 plus 4 plus 6, or any rearrangement of these numbers such as 6 plus 2 plus 4; or two pieces could move, one piece by 2 spaces and the other piece by 4 plus 6, or 6 plus 4, or any other combination desired; or three pieces could be moved one 2 spaces, one 4 spaces, and one 6 spaces, as long as each resting space was not blocked by enemy pieces.

3. The pieces were entered on the board in the first quarter and all travelled in the same direction.

4. If a player had two or more pieces on a space this space became barred to the enemy and the pieces were safe from capture. They were called *ordinarii* or *piled men.*

5. If a player moved a piece onto a space occupied by an enemy *vagi* (singleton) the latter was sent off the board and had to re-enter the game at the next possible throw.

6. Pieces unable to move because they were blocked by enemy ordinarii were known as *inciti.*

7. A player was forced to use the whole of his throw if this were possible, even if it was to the player's disadvantage: any part of a

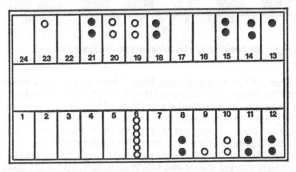

5. *A diagram of Zeno's disastrous throw at Tabula, c. A.D. 480, and recorded some fifty years later by Agathias of Myrine.*

throw which was unplayable was lost and the turn passed to his opponent.

Backgammon

Over the centuries Tabula became modified into Tables, known in England as Backgammon (figure 6). Occasionally Victorian or earlier boards may be found in antique shops, while new boards are on sale in the larger games shops, together with booklets of rules and instructions for play. In the Middle East the game is known as Tric-trac, and is often played in the streets on tables outside cafés.

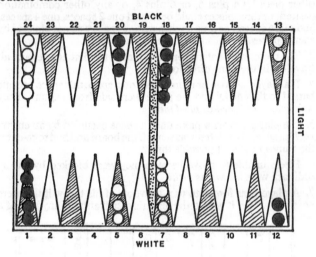

6. Opening position of the tablemen in Backgammon.

Some of the medieval table-boards were magnificent works of art. One found in the *mensa* of the altar of the diocesan church of St Valentine in Aschaffenburg in 1852 had been used as a reliquary. The plain points were pieces of red-veined oriental jasper, which were polished on their upper surfaces, the sides being inlaid, and the contrasting points were overlaid with thick pieces of split rock-crystal, themselves inlaid. Beneath were small terracotta figures, variously painted with green, red, yellow, blue, and white tints, on a gold ground. They represented twin-tailed sirens, dragon-like monsters and centaurs, and depicted battles between beasts and men. The spaces between the points were covered with thin silver-leaf impressed with leaves and other ornaments. At each end of the board were small drawers for holding the pieces, but these were missing.

Chasing the Girls

In contrast to the superb Aschaffenburg board, table-boards are still in use in isolated parts of Iceland the points of which are merely wooden strips tacked onto a plank, similar to the Tabula boards of the late Roman period. One of the Icelandic games, Chasing the Girls, may date back to this period.

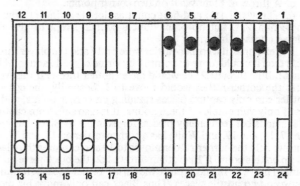

7. Opening position of the tablemen in Chasing the Girls.

Rules for Chasing the Girls

1. The players throw a single die and the lower scorer plays first.

2. Two cubic dice are thrown but only throws of 6: or 1:, or any doublet, are used. On throwing a doublet the player has another turn.

3. A throw of 6: 6: counts as a double doublet and the player may move four of his pieces six places each.

4. A throw of any other doublet permits the movement of two pieces the indicated number of spaces and the player has another turn.

5. A throw of 6: or 1: allows one piece to move this number of points.

6. No other throw scores.

7. All the pieces move in an anti-clockwise direction and continue

11

to circulate around the board until one player has lost all his pieces.

8. If a piece lands on a point occupied by an opponent's piece the latter is removed from the board.

9. Doubling up on a point is not allowed and if a throw brings a piece to a point on which the player already has a piece the former is placed on the first vacant point beyond.

10. When a player has only one man left, known as a *corner-rattler*, the method of play changes:

    a. The corner-rattler only lands on the corner points of the four quarters of the board; that is, on 1, 6, 7, 12, 13, 18, 19, and 24.

    b. A throw of 1: moves it on to the next corner point.

    c. A throw of 6: moves it on two corner points.

    d. Throws of 1:1: and 6:6: count as double a single throw of these numbers, but no other double counts except to give the player another throw.

For example, if a corner-rattler were on 16 and the player threw 6:1: then it would move to point 18 by virtue of the 1: and to 24 by the 6:. If he threw 2:2: he would have another throw. If this were 5:1: the corner-rattler would move to 1. Secondly, the corner-rattler can only capture pieces standing on corner points, and is itself only vulnerable on these points. It is also safe from capture if it stands between enemy pieces: for example, if Black has men on 17, 18, and 19, and White has a corner-rattler on 13, and White throws 3:1: the corner-rattler moves to 18 and captures the Black piece on this point. If Black then throws 1:2: the black piece on 17 cannot move to 18 and capture the corner-rattler because it stands between two hostile pieces. Thus Black can only move his piece which stands on 19 to 20, or his piece on 17 to 20, the next vacant point.

If Black threw 1:6:, however, the black piece on 19 could move to 1, using the 6: and then the black piece on 17 could move to 18 and capture White's corner-rattler and win the game.

Both players may be reduced to corner-rattlers when the game develops into a chase, and it may be a considerable time before one of them is beaten.

The Backgammon family of games, with an origin at least as early as the Royal Tombs of Ur (*c.* 3000 B.C.), spans some 5,000 years of constant use.

Nyout

The kingdom of Korea was founded in 1122 B.C. A board game called Nyout which is played there today in the taverns for money has survived virtually unchanged down the centuries. Written records exist showing that a variation of the game was being played in the third century A.D.

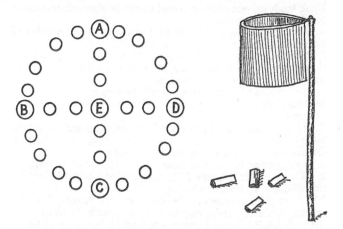

3. Nyout board, ring, and four pam-nyout.

The board consists of twenty-nine marks drawn on a piece of wood or paper, the one at the centre and those at the cardinal points being larger than the others. The mark at the top is the *ch'ut* (exit). The pieces represent horses, made of wood, stone or cardboard, and their movements are controlled by four dice known as *pam-nyout*. These are about one inch long, white and flat on one side and curved and blackened by charring on the other. To prevent cheating they are thrown through a ring of straw about two inches in diameter which is attached to a stick a foot or so long stuck into the ground. Scoring is made on the following basis:

Four black sides up—5 $\Big\}$ and the player has another turn.
Four white sides up—4
Three white sides up—3
Two white sides up—2
One white side up—1

If a pam-nyout falls in an upright position it counts as though it had fallen with a black side up.

Rules for Nyout

1. The players throw the pam-nyout in turn, the highest scorer becoming the leader and the others following in order of their scores.
2. Throwing a 5: or a 4: gives a player another throw which is made before moving his piece.
3. The players enter their horses on the mark to the left of the ch'ut, and move anti-clockwise according to their throws. If a

13

horse lands on one of the cardinal marks he short-circuits along two limbs of the cross.

4. The object of the game is to manoeuvre an agreed number of horses around the circle and out at the ch'ut.

5. If two persons play each has four horses; if three play each has three horses; and if four play the players sitting opposite are partners and have two horses each.

6. If a horse catches up with another belonging to the same player they may be doubled up as a team and moved round the circuit as one unit.

7. If a horse lands on a mark occupied by an opponent's horse the latter is kicked and must go back to the beginning and start again. On making a kick the player has an extra turn.

8. A player may move his partner's horses instead of his own.

9. When a player throws a 5: or a 4: and has a second throw he may divide it between two horses.

10. When a horse enters the board a throw of 5: takes it to the first cardinal mark and it may then move towards the ch'ut along the radii BE,EA. If the throw is less than 5:, but the next throw brings it to B, it may travel along the same course, otherwise the horse continues on towards B. If it lands on B it can travel along CE, EA; otherwise it must continue on towards A, the exit. Landing on D directs the horse along DE,EA which is further than continuing along the perimeter.

There is considerable evidence that in antiquity Nyout was taken to North America across the Berring Straits; similar Cross and Circle games, together with degenerate forms, are played by the North American Indians, the best known being Zohn Ahl. Boards cut into stone seats have been found in the ruins of the Mayan cities of Palenque and Chichen Itza.

Pachisi

Nyout also seems to have spread westwards, and was modified in India into Pachisi. Emperor Akbar played on courts of inlaid marble. In the centre was a dais four feet high on which the players sat, while sixteen young slaves from the harem wearing appropriately coloured dresses moved about the red and white squares of the board as directed by the throws of cowrie shells. Traces of these royal boards remain at Agra and Allahabad.

Modern boards sold in the bazaars are usually made of cloth, cut into the shape of a cross, and divided into squares with embroidery (figure 9).

The marked squares represent castles in which the pieces are safe from capture. A castle occupied by a player's piece is open to his partner's pieces, but closed to the enemy's. Each player has

14

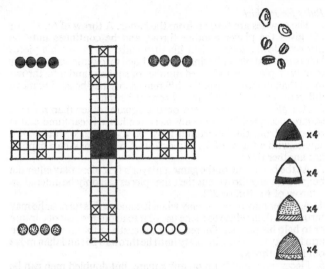

9. Pachisi board, pieces and six cowrie shells.

four beehive-shaped wooden pieces marked with his own colour although in more expensive sets these pieces are made from ivory. Six cowrie shells serve as dice and scoring is made on the following basis:

2 cowries with mouths up—2
3 cowries with mouths up—3
4 cowries with mouths up—4
5 cowries with mouths up—5
6 cowries with mouths up—6
1 cowrie with mouth up —10 } and another throw.
0 cowries with mouths up—25

The game is played by four players, each having four pieces. The players sitting opposite each other are partners, and yellow and black play against red and green. Each piece enters the game from the central space and travels down the middle of his own arm of the cross and then anti-clockwise around the board returning back up the middle row of his own arm to the central space. Pieces can only reach home by an exact throw and are then turned onto their side to show that they have completed the circuit.

15

Rules for Pachisi

1. The cowries are thrown from the hands. A throw of 6:, 10:, or 25: gives the player another throw, and he continues until he throws a lower score, when his turn ends. He moves his pieces before the next player begins his turn. Each throw allows the player to move a piece the indicated number of squares, and if he throws more than once in a turn, the different scores may be used to move different pieces. A single throw cannot be split.

2. If a player moves a piece onto a square, other than a castle square, occupied by an enemy piece the latter is captured and is removed from the board and must be re-entered on the centre square with a throw of 6:, 10:, or 25:. A player making a capture has another throw.

3. At the beginning of the game a player's first piece may enter the board with any throw, but the other pieces can only be entered on a throw of 6:, 10:, or 25:.

4. A player may refuse to play when it comes to his turn, or he may throw and then refuse to make use of it to avoid the risk of capture or to help his partner. On reaching the castle at the end of his own arm he may wait there in safety until he throws a 25: and then move out in one throw.

5. Pieces may double up on any square, but doubled men can be sent back to start again if they are hit by an equal or larger number of men belonging to the enemy, unless they are resting on a castle square.

Pachisi was modified and introduced into England under patent about 1896 as Ludo. The cowrie shells were replaced by a cubic die, and the pieces started their journey from outside the cross instead of from the centre. Ludo boards and rules are available from any games shop.

Georgian and Victorian race games

Antiquarian booksellers occasionally display Georgian and Victorian race games among their stock. Like early maps, these games were prints from engraved plates and were embellished by hand with water-colours, each copy varying a little at the discretion of the colourist. Shortly before 1840 lithography was introduced, but hand-colouring was often used to supplement the process. The illustration was then cut up into rectangles and mounted on linen, a method still used today for many road maps. The earlier games were usually inserted into a slipcase of thin cardboard which was covered with a marbled paper and a gummed title-label.

About 1800 folding covers of cardboard covered in cloth with titling in gold began to replace slipcases, a more durable method of protecting the games, and most of the best preserved specimens surviving today were guarded in this manner. Many of the older engravings show beautiful workmanship, preserving strange spellings and recording places now forgotten, or alternatively omitting cities now world famous.

F. R. B. Whitehouse lists two hundred and two of these games in his fascinating *Table Games of Georgian and Victorian Days*, many of which he illustrates and describes. This book has recently been republished. There is only space here to give an outline of '*The Royal Geographical Amusement* or *The Safe and Expeditious Traveller* through all the Parts of Europe by sea and by land: An instructive Game calculated for the Improvement of the Young Learners of Geography by Dr Journey. Published in June 1787 by Robert Sayer, map and printseller, 53 Fleet Street. Price 6/-. Completely done upon a past Board, (sic) with Box, Totum, Pillars and Counters included.' The first edition of this game was published in 1774.

The game was played with a tee-totum, markers (then called pillars) and counters with which the players paid any fines incurred on the journey which began at Calais, passed through France, Spain and Portugal, back into France, Switzerland, Italy, and then by sea to Athens (Greece at that time was part of the Turkish Empire in Europe). After Athens the players travelled by land to Constantinople (Istanbul), Hungary, Poland, Prussia, Courland (now Lithuania and part of Latvia), Moscow, Archangel and thence on a ship along the course taken by the Arctic convoys in the Second World War to Dronthen (Trondheim), Sweden, Norway, Denmark, Germany, the Netherlands and finally across the channel to London, the climax of the journey, and triumph for the first traveller home. One hundred and three towns were marked along the route with comments and instructions applying to each. A few examples are:

7. St Malo: a sea-port of Brittany. If it is late when you arrive take care of the twelve bull-dogs who guard its avenues in the night-time.

12. Bayonne: a sea-port town in the Labourd, renowned for its hams, its goose-quills, and its Jews.

17. Lisbon: the capital of Portugal. For fear of earthquakes, *autos da fé* and Portuguese ministers stay here as short a time as you can, and go directly to Seville, the next number.

32. Lyon: the second city of France. Stay one turn to see its silk manufactures, the first of Europe, and in which 100,000 persons are employed.

41. Farrara: a decayed and very unwholesome city in the Pope's dominions. The traveller must go back to Montpellier, No. 29, to breathe the pure air of that city.

51. Messina: till destroyed by the earthquake in 1784, was the

second city of Sicily, with a fine sea-port, and a great silk trade. It gives its name to a very famous strait.

54. Malta: a little rocky island, the chief place of the knights of the same name, the Don Quixotes of the Mediterranean.

76. St Petersberg: the metropolis of the Russian Empire. Stay one turn to consider the new Equestrian statue of Peter the First, and pay your compliments to the Empress.

78. Maelstrom: a dangerous whirlpool off the coast of Norway. Here the ship wherein you embarked at Archangel to go round Cape North is lost among the rocks. You have the good fortune to escape ashore, but lose the chance of the game.

82. Bergen: the capital of Norway, a sea-port of good trade.

85. Strelitz: the residence of Queen Charlotte's elder brother. Stay two turns to view the Duke of Mecklenburg's fine palace, and the town of Mirow, where Her Majesty was born.

89. Hanover: the capital of His Majesty's German dominions. Stay one turn to see the royal palace of Herrenhausen and then proceed on your journey to Amsterdam, No. 96.

93. Mentz: the capital of the electorate of that name, famous for its Rhenish wines, and for being the birthplace of John Gutenberg, who invented the art of printing in 1450.

96. Amsterdam: the capital of the Seven Provinces. Stay three turns to see the stadhouse, the arsenal, and the village of Sardam, famous for its ship builders.

102. Ostend: a sea-port in Austrian Flanders, where you must embark in the packet boat for Dover.

103. London: the capital of England, and metropolis of the British Empire. (The Game).

These race games fall into five groups: geographical, historical, instructional, moral teaching and pure entertainment. They can provide hours of pleasure and a magic carpet back into a world that is now history when travel was by stage-coach and sailing ship; Catherine the Great ruled Russia; the earthquake in Messina was still a recent disaster; the King of England was also Duke of Hanover; Amsterdam was the capital of the Seven Provinces; Austria held part of Flanders; and all writing was done with a quill pen.

Children must have learnt much without realising it—countries, rivers, towns, industries and peoples were all absorbed painlessly by candlelight in the evening around the nursery fire.

Some games were issued with a booklet giving additional information about the events portrayed in the little vignettes on the engraving. The first fourteen pages of the booklet issued with *The Jubilee*, published by J. Harris in 1810, was concerned with the game, but pages 15 to 54 were a tabulation of 'Remarkable Occurrences During the Reign of his Present Majesty'. Two extracts must suffice:

'The year 1780 was disgraced by riots in London. On this occasion a mob, supposed to consist of 50,000 persons, and headed by Lord George Gordon, marched to the House of Commons, and insulted many of the members; the chapels of the Sardinian and Bavarian ambassadors were demolished; the prisons of Newgate, the King's Bench, the Fleet and New Bridewell, were destroyed, and the prisoners liberated; the Bank of England was attempted; and a great number of houses were wrapped in flames, whilst another party of the rebels marched to cut off the pipes of the New River, and render abortive all attempts to extinguish the conflagration. For some time the Ministry remained inactive, and seemed to have been affected with no less terror than the citizens. But at length the military power was brought forward, Lord Gordon was apprehended, and order and tranquillity were restored. On the subsequent meeting of Parliament, his Majesty lamented the necessity he had been under of employing force to suppress the riots; and an address of thanks was unanimously voted.'

Under June 1809: 'Daniel Lambert died at Stamford, in the 40th year of his age. Upon being weighed, within a few days of his death he was found to be 52 stone, 11 lbs, (14 lbs to the stone) which is 10 stone 11 lbs more than the great Mr Bright of Malden ever weighed. His coffin was six feet four inches long, four feet four inches wide, and two feet four inches deep. It was built upon two axletrees and four clog wheels; and upon these the remains of this surprising man were drawn by eight men with ropes to the new burial-ground at the back of St Martin's church; the window and part of the wall of the room in which he lay, having been taken down to allow his exit.'

Pasang

Pasang was played by women in the kampongs of Brunei, especially during the night-long ceremonies attending circumcision, initiation, and marriage. Two, three or four players could take part. The board was made of hard wood, commonly kayu balian, mengaris, salangan batu or malangai. The playing surface was formed by a grid of scratched lines with the points of intersection converted into shallow cups. In the centre of the board occupying nine points was a store (*gadong*) about four and a half inches in diameter used to hold the balls (*buah*).

The board had a raised border one inch wide and half an inch high to protect the balls from accidental displacement during play. Pasang boards varied in size and the number of cups, depending upon the wood available: frequently they had eleven by eleven

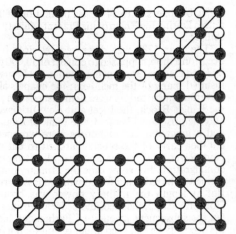

10. A pasang board of 11 by 11 lines (112 cups) set out for the opening known as 'Broken into pieces'. Original in the Brunei National Museum.

lines, making 121 points of intersection, but the central nine points were covered by the store, leaving 112 cups for play. There were 56 white balls over half an inch in diameter and worth two points (*kayu*). The same number of black balls were slightly smaller in diameter and worth one point.

One player arranged the balls on the board according to her fancy, or according to one of many recognised and named opening patterns: Broken into pieces (figure 10); Youth; Running cloud; Sticking flower; Flower in a vase; Chicken leg; Ascent to a palace; Composed flower.

When the initial arrangement of the pieces was complete the player called *kas* (start).

Rules for Pasang

1. The opening player began by lifting a ball from any of the four cups at the corners of the board and placing it into her store.
2. The turn of play then passed clockwise to the next player on her left, who lifted one of the three possible pieces to jump over a piece into the vacant cup. The piece passed over was lifted and placed in her store.
3. Pieces could only move by making a short leap. More than one short leap could be made in a single turn of play, and the capturing piece could change direction, including along a marked diagonal. As pieces were captured they were removed from the board.
4. A player could only capture one, three, five or seven balls in a turn of play. If two, four or six were at risk, the turn finished short of the last piece, only one, three or five being removed from the

board.

5. A player was not obliged to make all the captures possible in a move, nor to take the greater number of pieces if two or more formations were at risk. There was no huffing.

6. When no more captures were possible the game was finished, and any balls left in isolation were dead. The winner was the player holding the highest score in her store, white balls counting two points and black balls one point.

7. Each of the losing players paid the winner her total score. These debts were settled and then the winner set out the balls in a pattern of her choice. There was no settlement among the losers of a game.

8. When the board was set the player on the previous winner's left began the new game by lifting one of the corner balls.

2. WAR GAMES

Shaturanga

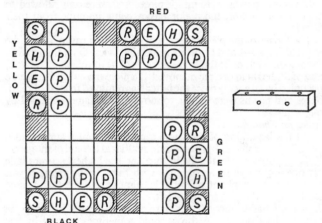

11. Shaturanga board, long die, and pieces arranged for the beginning of a game. P=pawn, S=ship, H=horse, E=elephant, R= rajah.

A race game called Ashta-pada, similar to Pachisi but using a square board of eight squares by eight, was played in Ancient India. About the fifth century A.D. this board was used for a new game, Shaturanga, which was a battle in miniature between four armies, each under the control of a rajah and each consisting of

21

four corps—infantry, cavalry, elephant troops and boatmen. Two of the forces were loosely allied against the other two. The pawns represented infantry; a horse the cavalry; an elephant the elephant troops; and a ship the boatmen. The rajah was represented by a human figure. Each piece had a different move:

The rajah moved one square orthogonally (by right-angles) or diagonally in any direction.

The elephant moved orthogonally forwards, sideways or backwards any number of unoccupied squares. He could not jump over a piece.

The horse moved one square orthogonally and one square diagonally, and could jump over intervening pieces (the knight's move in modern chess).

The ship moved two squares diagonally and could jump over an intervening piece.

The pawns moved one square orthogonally forwards, unless they were making a capture when they moved one square diagonally forwards.

Ships and pawns were minor pieces and were only allowed to capture each other, the major pieces being immune from their attack.

The moves of the pieces were decided by the throw of a long die marked 2:, 3:, 4: and 5: on its respective faces. On a throw of 2: the ship moved; of 3: the horse moved; of 4: the elephant moved; and of 5: the rajah or a pawn moved. If a piece moved onto a square occupied by an enemy piece the latter was removed from the board. Ships and pawns were unable to move onto squares occupied by major pieces.

Rules for Shaturanga

1. At the beginning of the game each player put a stake into a pool. This was shared by the victorious allies at the end of the game.
2. Each player threw the die in turn and the highest scorer made his opening move in accordance with this throw, unless it was a 4: when the elephant was unable to move and the turn passed clockwise to the player on the left.
3. A piece had to move if this were possible, even if it was to the player's disadvantage. A throw could sometimes be used by one of a choice of pieces; for example, if a 5: were thrown the rajah or a pawn could move, or if the ally's forces had been taken over, one of his pawns or the rajah.
4. If a player could not use a throw it was lost and the die was passed to the next player.
5. Seizing a throne: when a rajah occupied the throne of an enemy rajah he 'seized a throne' and won a single stake from the despoiled opponent. If he captured either enemy rajah at the same time he won a double stake. If a rajah mounted the throne of his ally he

assumed command of the allied forces as well as his own, and with his own or his partner's throws he could move either his own or his ally's pieces.

6. Regaining a throne: if a player whose ally's rajah had been captured, himself captured a hostile rajah, he could propose an exchange of captive rajahs with the player owning the remaining rajah, but the latter could refuse the exchange if he wished. Rescued rajahs re-entered the board on their own throne square, or if these were occupied, on the nearest vacant square.

7. If a player, whose rajah was still on the board but whose ally's rajah had been taken prisoner, captured both enemy rajahs he could claim the replacement of his ally's rajah without exchange or ransom.

8. Building an empire: a player who succeeded in seizing his ally's throne and in capturing both enemy rajahs had 'built an empire'. If the player's rajah made the capture on the hostile rajah's throne square he won a quadruple stake. If the player's rajah made the capture on some other square he won a double stake. If the capture of the second hostile rajah was made by any other piece the player won a single stake.

9. Concourse of shipping: each ship sailed on a different course controlling different squares, and they could not attack each other directly. But if three ships were on adjacent squares and the fourth moved into position to occupy the fourth square the player 'completed a concourse of shipping' and he captured the two enemy vessels and took control of the moves of his ally's ship. There were only five positions on the board where a concourse of shipping could occur.

10. Promotion of pawns: if a pawn reached an unmarked square on the opposite side of the board it was promoted to the piece of that square, either a horse or an elephant. Promotion only occurred, however, if the player had already lost one or more pawns. He was not allowed to have a promoted piece and three pawns on the board, and promotion was delayed until a pawn had been lost. A pawn reaching a marked square could take no further part in the game unless it became a 'privileged pawn'.

11. Privileged pawn: if a player had only a ship and a pawn left, this pawn became privileged and on reaching any square on the opposite side of the board it was promoted to any piece at the choice of its owner.

12. Drawn game: if a player lost all his pieces except his rajah he was considered to have fought to an honourable peace and the game was drawn.

When gambling became forbidden by law, shaturanga players evaded punishment by discarding the die, thus removing the element of luck, and the game became one of skill. Other changes followed. Each pair of allied armies was combined into a single force, one of the kings being reduced to the rank of a prime minister with his power of movement restricted to one square diagonally backwards or forwards. The moves of the ship and the elephant were transposed, the elephant moving diagonally two squares, while the ship assumed the powerful orthogonal moves of the ancient elephant. The game ceased to be shaturanga; it had developed into a medieval form of chess known as shatranj.

A modern chess set can be adapted to play shaturanga by tying a red ribbon around half the black pieces, and a green ribbon around half the white. This will give four armies; Black, Red, Green, and White. Alternatively half the pieces may be painted, but this will spoil them for playing the standard game.

Burmese chess

The forms of chess played today in countries east of India become more and more removed from the original Shatranj as one travels towards Japan. As far as possible familiar names of pieces are used, but if there is no equivalent then the piece is called by its English translation.

In Burmese chess the board of eight squares by eight is usually unchequered and with the long diagonals clearly marked. It forms the upper surface of a shallow box equipped with drawers to hold

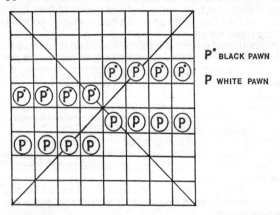

P˙ BLACK PAWN

P WHITE PAWN

12. Burmese chess board with the pawns in their opening positions. The pieces behind the pawns can be placed on any squares the players choose.

the chessmen which are always carved figures, though often of crude workmanship.

After the initial placing of the pieces at the beginning of the game, and there are several well-known formations, the players are permitted to adjust their major pieces by abnormal moves in alternate turns of play until one player moves a pawn, when both players must then continue with the legal moves of the chessmen. Any pawn moving onto a square on either of the long diagonals can be promoted to a queen if the player has no queen on the board. When promoted the new queen may occupy the pawn's square, or any adjacent square not threatened by an opposing piece.

Moves of pieces

Pawns move one square forwards, but capture one square diagonally forwards.

Bishops move one square backwards or forwards along a diagonal, or one square orthogonally forwards.

Knights move one square orthogonally and one square diagonally —they have the same power of leaping over a piece as in European chess.

Rooks move orthogonally any number of unoccupied squares.

The queen moves one square diagonally backwards or forwards.

The king moves one square in any direction.

Stalemate is not permitted; a player must leave his opponent an opening for play.

The shorter moves of the pieces brings them into intimate contact and creates a feeling of the mêlèe of battle which is lost in

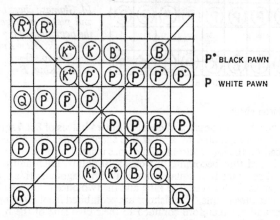

P° BLACK PAWN

P WHITE PAWN

13. Burmese chess showing two popular initial formations.

European chess where power develops on key squares often at some distance from the pieces controlling them.

Siamese chess

Siamese chessboards are unchequered and the opening position of the pawns is peculiar to this variety of the game. The end of the game tends to be tedious and to lessen this special rules relate to a solitary king. When a player has only the king left his opponent must secure checkmate within a prescribed number of moves, the number depending upon the strength of the opponent's pieces. If he fails to achieve checkmate in the number of moves permitted, the game is drawn.

BLACK

14. Siamese chess board and pieces arranged at the beginning of a game. R=Rook, Kt=Knight, B=Bishop, Q=Queen, K=King, P=Pawn.

WHITE

Chinese chess

The Chinese chessboard consists of two halves of 8 x 4 squares which are separated by a river one square wide. The pieces are placed on the intersections of the lines instead of on the squares, the board thus becoming one of 9 x 10 points. Each half of the board contains four squares marked with diagonals; this area is known as the fortress. The king and the two queens are restricted to these nine points. The bishops are prohibited from crossing the river and are therefore confined to their own side of the board. The other pieces are free to move anywhere.

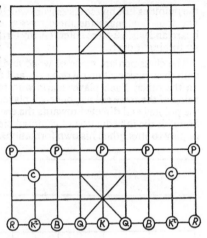

15. Chinese chessboard with one player's pieces arranged for the start of a game. Note the 'river' across the middle of the board and the presence of two Queens.

RED KING

The chessmen are circular discs with the ranks written on the upper face, in red for one side and in green for the other. There is a unique piece found only in Chinese chess, the cannon, which moves orthogonally in any direction, but which, when capturing, must jump over some piece on the way to the point being attacked. The intervening piece is known as a screen, and can belong to either side. Cannons cannot jump unless they make a capture and can only jump over one piece at a time. If a cannon is threatening attack and the screen is moved, the threat disappears. The interposition of a second piece between the cannon and its prey has the same effect.

Chinese chess is regarded as the national game of Hong Kong, and one of the television channels there devotes a considerable portion of its viewing time to recording championship matches.

Sho-gi

The strangest and most modified form of chess is Sho-gi. The Generals' Game, or Japanese chess, is played on a little table with its upper surface marked with a rectangle divided into eighty-one smaller rectangles. The pieces are placed on the spaces and not on

27

the points as in Chinese chess from which it was probably derived. The four dots mark the three rows at each player's end of the board and when a piece enters enemy territory it may be promoted by turning it over.

The chessmen are made of wood and shaped like little coffins with their rank written on one side, and the rank after promotion on the other. Each player starts with twenty pieces, both sides being of the same colour, but each player's pieces are placed with the pointed end directed towards the enemy. A unique feature of Sho-gi is the introduction of captured pieces by a player in a turn of play to strengthen his own formations.

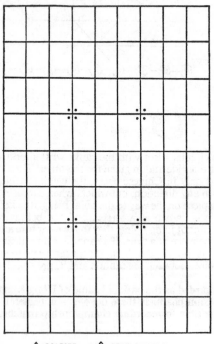

SOLDIER   GOLD GENERAL

16. A Japanese chessboard, and the upper and underneath surfaces of a pawn.

There are about ten million Sho-gi players in Japan, and every year there is a title match, the Meijin-sen, between the reigning champion and his leading challenger. Only the best equipment is used in these encounters: the boards made of torreya wood, the pieces of boxwood, and a pair of small side-tables of mulberry to hold the captures—in all costing some £500.

Gala

Peculiar forms of chess are not confined to the Orient.

Gala, or Farmers' chess, was once popular in Dithmarschen, Schleswig-Holstein, though now it is virtually forgotten. Only a few antique boards still exist in remote farmhouses, but readers can easily make one of their own (figure 17). The board of 10 x 10 chequered squares is similar to that used for Continental Draughts (figure 24), except for the marking of a central cross with *deflection-lines;* pieces crossing them change direction as explained below.

Each player starts with twenty pieces: two kings, five rooks, five bishops and eight pawns. These pieces were all the same shape, like small skittles, twenty white ones for one player and twenty black for the other. The ranks were indicated by colouring the upper halves of the pieces; those of bishops were red and those of

BLACK

WHITE

17. Farmers' chess played on a 10 x 10 cells board. Each player has twenty pieces arranged at the beginning of the game in the four corners of the board.

29

rooks were green while the kings, which were slightly larger than the other pieces, had their upper halves gold. The pawns remained unpainted.

The object of the game was to capture both opposing kings.

Moves of the pieces

The pawns moved diagonally up to the deflection-line or to the first square beyond it, remaining on the same colour, but after this move they could only move one square at a time in any direction, including backwards. If a pawn returned to the original pawn starting line its next move could only be diagonally forwards, as at the beginning of the game.

The rooks moved orthogonally in any direction for any number of squares, but on crossing a deflection-line their course was deflected and they moved diagonally to the next deflection-line, i.e. one square diagonally on. The whole movement could be completed as one turn of play. Alternatively, the rook could stop on any square along the route. The next move after the diagonal deflection in the deflection-zone continued orthogonally as far as desired, or until meeting another deflection-line.

The bishops moved diagonally any number of squares in any direction until crossing a deflection-line when, after the first square behind the first deflection-line and until meeting another deflection-line, they travelled orthogonally and then, after crossing the second deflection-line, diagonally again.

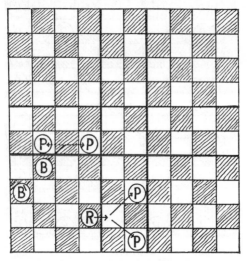

18. The method of capture by a Bishop and a Rook when crossing a deflection line. The Bishop B can only capture the Pawn on the right. A Bishop on B¹ could capture either pawn.

The kings moved one square at a time in any direction and were not affected by the deflection-lines. If a king reached one of the four squares in the centre of the cross formed by the deflection-lines, he could be placed at the next move on any free square on the board, excluding the forty squares occupied by pieces at the beginning of the game. At times this was a valuable privilege.

Capturing

Kings, rooks and bishops could capture when passing over deflection-lines, but the pawns could not. The bishop's power of capture over a deflection-line was limited, however, by a rule that if it was standing on a square next to a deflection-line it could not capture a piece standing on the adjacent square over the line (figure 18).

If a player made a move threatening a king he was required to call 'Gala'; the opponent was then compelled to move the threatened piece if possible to safety. If he were unable to do so, when the king was captured at the next move, the game continued until one player had lost both his kings when play ended. If only two opposing kings were left on the board the game was drawn.

(Translated from a German text by Mr M. C. Oswald.)

Four Field Kono

Four Field Kono is played in Korea, each player having eight pieces of his own colour arranged on a board as in figure 19. Black moves first. The pieces capture by jumping over one of their own pieces onto an enemy piece standing on the point immediately beyond. When not making a capture the pieces move orthogonally one point at a time, the players moving their pieces alternately. The object of the game is to capture or block the opponent's force.

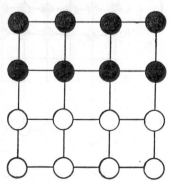

19. Board and pieces at the beginning of a game of Four Field Kono.

Surakarta

Surakarta takes its name from the ancient town of Surakarta in Java. Each player had twelve pieces, usually stones for one side and shells for the other, and the board was drawn in the sand.

Rules for Surakarta

1. The opening position is shown in figure 20 with the pieces arranged on the points of intersection.
2. The players draw lots or cast a die for the advantage of first move.
3. The pieces move one point at a time in any direction, forwards, backwards, sideways or diagonally, but are not permitted to jump over another piece, nor to land on an occupied point, except when making a capture as described under rule 4.

Examples of movement of pieces: stone from D2 to E3 (Diagonal); shell from E5 to E4 (Forwards); stone from C2 to D2 (Sideways); and shell from E4 to E5 (Backwards).

4. The method of capture appears to be unique. This is only permitted after the piece has travelled along one of the eight circular lines, and it must enter and leave the three-quarters of a circle along a line at a tangent.

The following example illustrates the way in which a capture is made and for the purposes of the example the positioning of the pieces is a stone on A1, C1, F1, E2, A3, C3, and E5, and a shell on B4, E4, A5, F5, A6, B6, E6, and F6.

If it were the stone's turn to play the following captures could

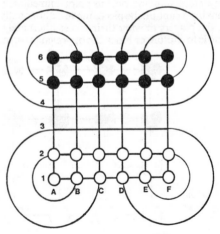

20. Board and pieces at the beginning of a game of Surakarta.

be made: from C3 to C6, circle to A4 and take the shell on B4; or from C3 to F3, circle to D1, D6, circle to F4 and take the shell on E4; or from E2 to F2, circle to E1 and take the shell on E4; or from E2 to A2, circle to B1 and take the shell on B4.

If it were the shell's turn to play there would be the following alternative captures: from B4 to A4, circle to C6 and take the stone on C3; or from E4 to F4, circle to D6, to D1, circle to F3, and take the stone on C3; or from B4 to B1, circle to A2 and take the stone on E2

The circles are only used when making a capture.

5. At the end of the game the winner's pieces remaining on the board are counted and recorded as points towards an agreed total for victory.

(Translated from a French text by Miss Fiona Brookes.)

Alquerque

An Arabic work known as the *Kitab-al Aghani,* written in the tenth century A.D., mentions a game called Quirkat. When the Moors invaded Spain they took El-quirkat with them and it is recorded in the Alfonso X manuscript, A.D. 1251-1282, under its Spanish name of Alquerque.

The opening position of the pieces in alquerque is shown in figure 21. The following rules are taken from the Alfonso manuscript which is now in the library of the monastery of St Lorenzo del Escorial, outside Madrid.

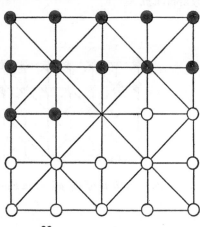

21. Opening positions of the pieces in Alquerque.

33

Rules for Alquerque

1. A piece may move from any point to any adjacent empty point along a line.
2. If the adjacent point is occupied by an enemy piece and the next point beyond it on the line is empty, the player's piece can make a short jump over the hostile piece which is removed from the board.
3. If another piece is then threatened it is also taken in the same turn of play by a second short leap, a change of direction being permitted.
4. Two or more pieces may be captured in this way in one move.
5. If a piece can make a capture, it must do so, otherwise it is *huffed* and removed from the board.
6. When one player has lost all his pieces his opponent has won the game.

Fanorona

This game from Madagascar was developed from Alquerque in about 1680 by doubling the board, increasing the number of pieces to forty-four and changing the method of capture.

Rules for Fanorona

1. White starts and moves a piece along any line to an adjacent empty point.
2. If the move ends on a point in contact with a point or points beyond in the line of movement occupied by enemy pieces in unbroken sequence, these are captured and removed. This is capture by approach.

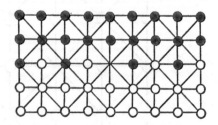

22. Opening positions of the pieces in Fanorona.

3. Capture may also be by withdrawal. If a player's piece moves away from a point contiguous with a point or points occupied by enemy pieces in the line of movement these pieces are removed from the board.

4. Captures are compulsory, but on the first move by each player only one sequence can be taken.

5. On the second and later moves a player may make several captures, either by approach or withdrawal, but each move must be along a different marked line; the piece must change direction to make each capture.

6. If a move places enemy pieces in two directions at risk of capture, the player can choose to remove pieces in either direction, but not in both. He is not compelled to capture the larger number.

7. The game ends when one player has lost all his pieces.

The second game is played differently with a *vela* opening. The defeated player starts and the previous winner sacrifices piece after piece until he has lost seventeen; at the same time he refrains from making any captures, and his opponent may only take one piece at each move. When seventeen pieces have been lost, normal play is resumed using the standard rules given above.

The third game is standard, and the fourth a vela game, each type of opening being played alternately.

Draughts

About A.D. 1100 a new game was invented, probably in the south of France, using Backgammon tablemen on a chequered chess-

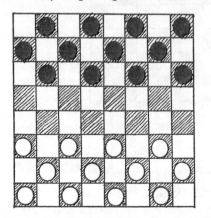

23. Opening positions of the pieces in English Draughts.

board with the Alquerque method of capture. Each player had twelve pieces called *ferses,* the name of the queens in medieval chess. The ferses in the new game moved in the same way as in the old, one square diagonally in any direction, and captured by a short leap diagonally.

Philip Mouskat (A.D. 1243) refers in his *Chronique* (lines 23617-20) to a king, indicating that a fers could be promoted to this rank. There was no compulsion to capture a threatened enemy piece, a survival of chess practice. When a compulsion rule was introduced about 1535 the old non-huffing game became known as Jeu Plaisant, in contrast to the huffing game Jeu Forcé. Modern English draughts is the jeu forcé of the sixteenth century. Boards, pieces and rules are obtainable at any games shop.

Continental draughts

Early in the eighteenth century a new game known as Continental draughts was being played in the cafés of Paris. The first book describing it was published in 1727 by Quercetane, a pseudonym, and was probably written about five years earlier.

Rules for Continental draughts
1. A chequered board of a hundred squares is used, and each player has twenty pieces arranged as in figure 24.

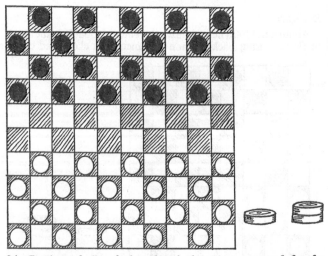

24. Continental draughtsboard with the pieces arranged for the beginning of a game. At the right is a man and a King.

2. A man moves one square diagonally forwards.

3. A man captures by a short leap diagonally forwards or backwards. Capturing is compulsory.

4. A king can move diagonally any number of unoccupied squares.

5. A king may land any number of vacant squares beyond a captured piece.

6. A king may combine the moves detailed in rules 4 and 5 to make a long leap.

7. Captured pieces are only lifted at the end of a move, and a dead piece forms an impassable barrier.

8. If a player has a choice of captures he must choose the one in which the greatest number of captures are made unless equal numbers are at risk, when the player has the choice of which pieces he will capture.

9. A man is only promoted to be a king if he remains on the opponent's back line; if on reaching the crownhead more captures are possible, they must be made and the move completed, when the man remains unpromoted until he again reaches the crownhead and remains there at the end of a move.

10. When a player has no pieces left on the board he has lost the game.

Reversi

This game was invented in 1888 and is played on a draughts board of sixty-four squares with sixty-four pieces which are black on one side and red on the other. Black begins by placing a piece black side up on one of the four central squares on the empty board. Red replies by placing his first piece red side up on another central square. These four squares are covered in the first four turns of play and then the players continue alternately, placing their pieces on a square adjacent to one occupied by an enemy piece. Any enemy pieces directly intervening between this piece and another of the player's own colour, orthogonally or diagonally, are captured and are turned over to expose the player's colour uppermost. A piece may change owners many times in the course of a game. When all the squares on the board are covered with pieces the player with most of his colour showing wins the game.

Ming Mang

The board for this Tibetan game is variable in size, but similar to a Go board without the specially marked points (figure 41).

Rules for Ming Mang

1. Each player lines up his counters on the points of two contigu-

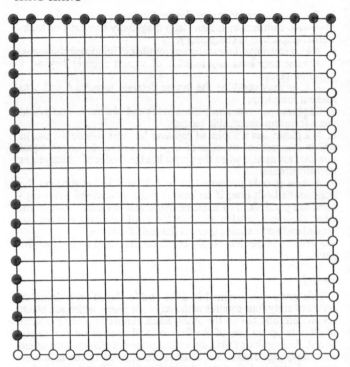

25. Board for Ming Mang, with the pieces arranged at the beginning of a game.

ous sides of the board. The number of pieces used depends upon the size of the board.

2. Each player moves one piece by alternate turns of play orthogonally to any vacant point along a line. Jumping is not permitted.

3. All captured pieces are replaced by pieces of one's own colour.

4. A piece is captured if it is trapped between two enemy pieces along a straight line. This rule applies to any number of contiguous pieces in a straight line, with an enemy piece at both ends, when the trapped pieces are removed from the board and replaced by pieces of the successful player's colour.

5. If a player has two pieces in a straight line with an empty point between them, his opponent may move a piece onto this point without it being captured. If the player then moves one of his

pieces away in any direction, on the next move he may return to the original point and capture his opponent's piece.

6. Pieces in the corners of the board cannot be captured because they cannot be trapped between enemy pieces in a straight line. The corners are crucial points, and if a player loses them he is likely to lose the game.

(This account is presented through the courtesy of the Venerable Trungpa Rinpoche of the Tibetan Centre, Eskdalemuir, Dumfriesshire. He ended his description with the remark: 'I do not think it is possible to find a Ming Mang set in this country. We use a Go board.')

For those without a Go board, a draughtsboard with thirty white and thirty black buttons makes an acceptable substitute. The pieces are placed on the squares and not on the points, as the chequering causes confusion (figure 26).

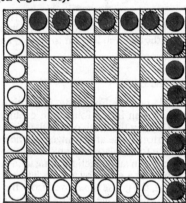

26. Ming Mang played on a draughtsboard.

Lambs and Tigers

Pulijudam, or the Tiger game, is popular with Hindu children throughout India.

Rules for Lambs and Tigers

1. One player has three tigers and the other fifteen lambs.
2. The pieces are introduced onto the points by alternate moves of play. When the three tigers have been placed on the marked points they can then move along a line to the nearest point, or jump over a lamb by a short leap, in which case the latter is removed from the board.
3. When all the lambs have been placed on the board, and only then, they may also move to any adjacent point along a line.

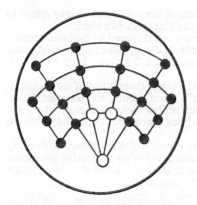

27. *A board for Lambs and Tigers. The Tigers (white pieces) are placed on the three points nearest the apex. The fifteen Lambs are placed on any of the twenty black points.*

4. The lambs try to hem in the tigers and prevent them moving, while the tigers endeavour to destroy and eat the lambs (figure 27).

Fox and Geese

Hala-tafl, the Fox game, is mentioned in the Icelandic *Grettis saga* written in the fourteenth century by an anonymous priest who lived in the north of the island.

Thirteen geese are arranged on the board as shown in figure 28 and the fox is placed on any vacant point. The fox and the geese can move in any direction along a line to the next point. If the fox jumps over a goose by a short leap and lands on an empty point ceyond, the goose is removed from the board. Two or more geese ban be killed in one move by a series of short leaps by the fox. The

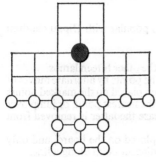

28. *Board and pieces arranged for the beginning of a game of Fox and Geese.*

geese cannot jump over the fox, but they try to crowd him into a corner and deprive him of the power to move. If they succeed he loses the game, but if he can deplete the geese until this is impossible then he is the winner.

The player moving the geese must win if he plays correctly. In later forms of the game the geese were increased to seventeen, but were unable to move backwards.

Fox and Geese is one of a series of Norse games in which sides of unequal strength, and with different powers of movement or mode of capture, struggle to achieve different objectives.

Tablut

When Linnaeus, the Swedish botanist, visited Lapland in 1732, he described the game of Tablut which was played by his hosts. A grid of 9 x 9 squares was marked out on a board, the central one being known as the *konakis* or throne. Only the Swedish king, who was larger than the other pieces, could occupy this square. One player had eight white Swedish soldiers and their king; the other had sixteen black Muscovites which were placed on the other marked squares (figure 29).

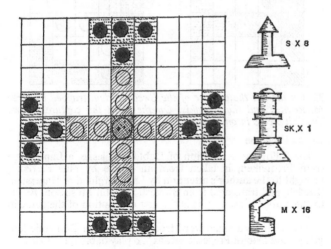

29. *Tablut board and pieces arranged at the beginning of a game. Swedish soldier, Swedish king and Muscovite shown at the right.*

Rules for Tablut

1. All the pieces move orthogonally any number of vacant squares.

2. A piece is captured and removed from the board when opposing pieces occupy both adjacent squares in a row or column (figure 30). A piece may move safely onto an empty square between two enemy pieces.

3. The king is captured if all four squares around him are occupied by enemy pieces, or if he is surrounded on three sides and the fourth is the konakis. When the king is captured the Muscovites are victorious.

4. If the king reaches any square on the periphery of the board the Swedes win. When there is a clear route for the king to a perimeter square the player must warn his opponent by saying 'Raichi'. When there are two clear routes he must say 'Tuichi', which is the equivalent of 'Checkmate', since it is impossible to block two directions in one move.

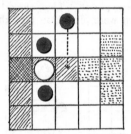 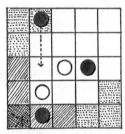

30. On the left the capture of the Swedish king, trapped by three Muscovites and the Konakis. On the right the capture of two Swedish pieces in one move.

Dablot Prejjesne

The following description of Dablot Prejjesne, a Lapp game from Frostviken, is taken from an article by Nils Keyland, brought to the author's attention by Lars Berglund of Hagersten, Sweden, and translated from Swedish by John Mosesson. As far as the author is aware this is the first description of the game in English.

'Dablo' is an archaic word from the northern Germanic language, and Dablot Prejjesne means 'To play dablo on a board'.

The board seen by Keyland was a fir-plank twenty inches long, twelve inches wide and one inch thick, the marked-out playing area being twelve inches by ten inches and divided into thirty squares with their diagonals, creating seventy-two points. The

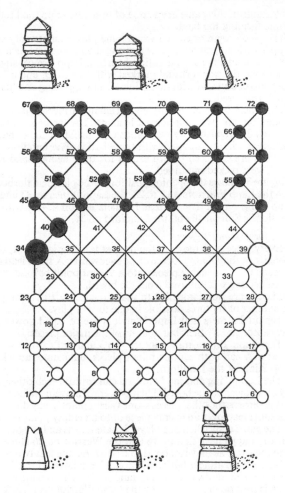

31. *Dablot Prejjesne board with the pieces arranged at the beginning of a game. At the top are the Lapp King, Lapp Prince, and a Lapp Warrior; below, a Tenant Farmer, Landlord's Son, and Landlord.*

43

contestants in this game are a tribe of nomadic Lapps and settled people farming the land.

The pieces were of carved wood. One player had twenty-eight Lapp Warriors, painted yellow and standing about one inch high with pointed helmets. In addition he had a Lapp Prince, slightly larger than the warriors and marked with two rings, and a Lapp King, larger still and with three rings. The Lapp King and his son were uncoloured.

The other player had twenty-eight Tenant Farmers an inch high, painted red and wearing horned helmets. The larger Landlord's Son was distinguished by two bands and his father the Landlord was larger still and marked with three bands. The Landlord and his son were coloured brown except for their helmets and rings which were picked out in red.

Figure 31 shows the opening position of the pieces on the board, with the Lapp Warriors on 1 to 28, the Lapp Prince on 33 and the Lapp King on 39. The Tenant Farmers are on 45-72, with the Landlord's Son on 40 and the Landlord on 34.

Rules for Dablot Prejjesne

1. Every piece may move to the nearest unoccupied point, orthogonally or diagonally, forwards or backwards. A short leap may be made over an enemy piece onto a vacant point beyond, when the passed piece is removed from the board.

2. Players are not compelled to make a capture, or to complete the number of captures possible in one turn of play.

3. Tenant Farmers and Lapp Warriors are of equal power and may capture each other, but not one of the major pieces.

4. The Lapp Prince may capture the Landlord's Son, or vice versa; they can both capture minor pieces, but cannot attack the Lapp King or the Landlord.

5. The Lapp King and the Landlord can capture each other, and any other piece on the board. Their powers of movement, however, are the same as the other pieces—one vacant point in any direction, or a short leap over an enemy piece onto an empty point beyond.

6. The game ends when one player is defenceless and resigns.

If the Lapps have first move and the Warrior on 26 is used to open the game he may rest on 31, 32, or 37. On the first two points he is safe from attack, but on 37 he can be removed if the Tenant Farmer on 48 jumps over him to land on 26. The Tenant Farmer on 26 is then open to capture by the Lapp Warrior on 15, 20 or 21 because points 37, 31 and 32 are vacant.

Figure 32 shows a game in progress in which eight Lapp Warriors and the Lapp King have been lost, while only one Tenant Farmer is off the board. It is the farmers' turn to play and, by moving the Landlord's Son on 38 with a short leap to 16, the Lapp

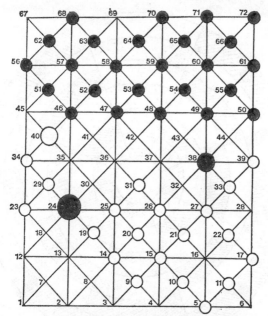

32. A game in progress. It is the Farmers' turn of play.

Warrior on 27 is removed. He may then move to 4, capturing the
warrior on 10, and then to 6, capturing the warior on 5. From
there he moves to 16, from 16 to 28 and finally back to his starting
point on 38, capturing warriors on 11, 22 and 33 on the way. Thus
he captures six Lapp Warriors in one move. A similar result would
have followed the moves 38-28-16-6-4-16-38.

7. If one player has only a major piece left, and the other has
several minor pieces, the latter can win the game by surrounding
the former and depriving him of the power to move. This is winning by immobilisation.

8. If the players are left with only one piece each of equal power,
either a Lapp Warrior and a Tenant Farmer or the Lapp Prince
and the Landlord's Son, one of the players calls for single combat,
when the pieces are moved towards each other in direct confronta-
tion when one piece with the move will capture the other. This
avoids a draw through an endless and futile chase.

9. If only the Lapp King and the Landlord are left on the board
the game is declared drawn.

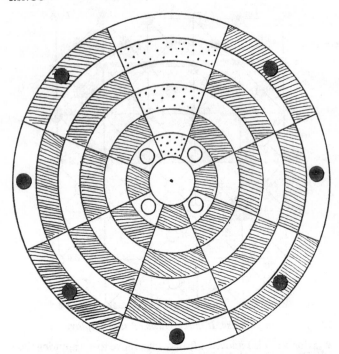

33. A Ringo board with the pieces in position at the beginning of a game.

Ringo

Ringo is played on the round board shown in figure 33. White places his four defenders on the white spaces of the innermost ring while Black places his seven attackers on the seven spaces of the outer ring, leaving the neutral zone empty.

Rules for Ringo

1. Only one piece may occupy a space at a time, with the exception of the citadel (*see* rule 17).
2. Both players move their pieces by moves or jumps.
3. Black's pieces can only move one space at a time towards the centre, and thus their progress alternates in colour from a black space onto a white, and vice versa. In the neutral zone they move from white to grey spaces.

46

4. White's pieces also move from one ring to the next, but can move backwards as well as forwards.

5. Pieces of either colour can jump over an opposing piece, landing on a vacant space immediately beyond. This is by a short leap onto the empty space of the same colour. The opposing piece is then captured and removed from the board.

6. Pieces of either colour can also land on top of an enemy piece, when the latter is also removed from the board.

7. Only one piece may be captured in any turn of play.

8. It is not compulsory to take a piece that is at risk.

9. In addition to the radial movement of the pieces, they may also move circumferentially along the ring on which they stand. Black is only permitted to move to the next adjacent space but White's defenders can move any number of empty spaces circumferentially, and can also make a long leap over a black piece landing immediately beyond. The latter is removed from the board. However, rules 10, 11, 12, 13 and 14 should be noted.

10. Pieces of either colour can move into the neutral zone, but have to wait for another turn of play before leaving it. It therefore acts as a barrier to White making a complete circular movement around the board.

11. A piece may make a capture when moving into the neutral zone.

12. A piece of either colour is not permitted to make a capture when leaving the neutral zone.

13. A piece in the neutral zone is safe from attack by an enemy piece.

14. Neither player can attack an opposing piece with a piece in the neutral zone.

15. Black is only permitted the same number of pieces in the neutral zone as White has left on the board.

16. White is not permitted to move a piece into the citadel.

17. Black wins the game if he places two of his pieces in the citadel when they are safe from attack. One black piece in the citadel is vulnerable to a white piece jumping over it.

18. Black can capture a white piece by jumping over it into the citadel.

19. White wins the game if he captures all the black pieces, or if he blocks their movement.

The following tactical points should be remembered. Firstly, Black should make use of the neutral zone to organise an assault on the citadel in safety. Secondly, White should try to leave one piece on the innermost ring to defend the citadel. He may capture a single black piece in the citadel by jumping over it.

(Translated from a German text by Mr M. C. Oswald.)

47

Pong hau k'i

Pong hau k'i comes from Canton in China. Each player has two stones of his own colour, which are placed as in figure 34, and one stone is moved at alternate turns of play along any line to the next empty point. If a player blocks his opponent and prevents him moving, the latter has lost the game.

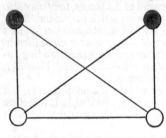

34. Pong hau k'i board and pieces at the beginning of a game.

Mu Torere

Mu Torere appears to be the only board game played by the Maori and the main participants are the Ngati Porou tribe on the east coast of the North Island of New Zealand. The board consists

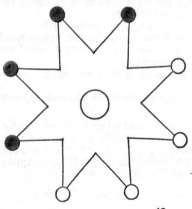

35. Mu Torere board and pieces at the beginning of a game.

of an eight-sided star with a central point or *putahi*. Each player has four pieces of his own colour which are placed on four adjacent points on the arms of the star. The players take it in turn to move first at the beginning of a game. The object is to block the opposing pieces so that they cannot move.

Rules for Mu Torere
1. Black begins and the players move alternately.
2. Only one piece is allowed on each point.
3. Jumping is not permitted.
4. There are three possible forms of move:
   a. A piece may move from one of the arms to an adjacent empty arm.
   b. From the putahi to an arm.
   c. From one of the arms to the putahi, provided that one or both the adjacent arms are occupied by an enemy piece or pieces.

Achi

Achi is played by Ghanese school-children, the board being marked out on the ground, and eight stones of two contrasting colours used as pieces.

In the first phase the stones are introduced onto any point in alternate turns of play. When the eight stones are in position the second phase begins, the players moving one stone one point along a line at each turn of play in an attempt to obtain three stones in a row. The first to achieve this is the winner.

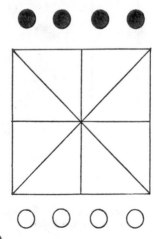

36. An empty Achi board at the beginning of a game. The stones are placed on any vacant point in alternate turns of play.

4

Nine Men's Morris

This game has been played for more than three thousand years. A board cut into a roofing slab at Kurna in Egypt shows that workmen building the temple there played the game around 1400 B.C. Two other boards were cut into the flight of steps at Mihintale in Ceylon by the masons who built the thirty-foot wide stairway in the first few years of the Christian era. In Asia Minor the design has been found in the first city at Troy and a morris-board was among the personal possessions of the king buried in the Gokstad Viking-ship about A.D. 900.

Rules for Nine Men's Morris
STAGE ONE

1. The two players have nine men each and enter them on the board at alternate turns of play onto any vacant point.

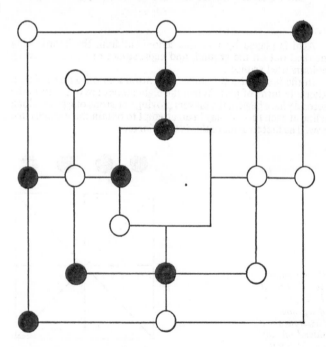

37. A Nine Men's Morris game at the end of the first stage with all the pieces on the board.

2. Each time a player forms a row or *mill* of three pieces along a line he removes one of his opponent's pieces from the board, but not one which is in a mill.

STAGE TWO

3. When all the men have been entered, the turns continue by moving a piece onto an adjacent vacant point along a line, with the object of making a mill and capturing an enemy piece.

4. A player blocking all his opponent's men so that they cannot move, or reducing him to two pieces, wins the game.

Renju

Renju, pronounced Rendzu, is the official name of the game popularly known as Gomoku-narabe, and means in Japanese to 'link round stone'. The popular name translated is 'five small round pieces to put side by side'. The board and pieces used in this game are the same as those used in I-go (Go) (figure 41). Although Renju does not hold the popular appeal of Go, or Sho-gi (Japanese chess), there are a few professionals and some of the popular weekly journals have a Renju corner where problems are presented and discussed (figure 38).

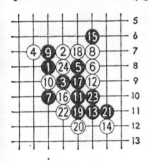

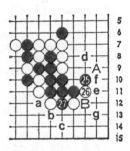

PROBLEM   SOLUTION

38. A Renju problem and solution taken from a daily newspaper and sent to the author by Mr K. Yano of Kobe, Japan. The problem is: which is the right position for the Black's next stone in order to arrive at a 4.3 fork? Answer: Black 25—because: Bl.25, Wh.26, Bl.27, and after that if (28) Wh. A, then (29) Bl. a→b,c, i.e. a 4.3 fork attained; or if (28) Wh. b, then (29) Bl. d→A. Remark: it seems as if Black wins easily with his next stone at e (→Wh.26, Bl. f and so forth). But for the Black's e, White responds with 26 instead of 27, and Black comes into a difficult situation.

Rules for Renju

1. The board of 19 x 19 points is empty at the beginning of the game, and the players place their pieces by alternate turns of play on any unoccupied point.

2. Players are not permitted to construct open-ended forks whose branches consist of three stones each. Forks of three and four, or four and four, are allowed.

3. The first player to form a contiguous line of five pieces on a row, column, or diagonal wins the game.

The game usually ends with each player placing thirty to forty stones.

Renju was introduced into Europe about 1885 and is known in England as Spoil Five. The pieces are placed on the squares and not on the points, and there are slight changes in the rules.

This account of Renju differs considerably from that of Gomoku given in the author's *Board and Table Games of Many Civilizations* (Volume I: 2nd Edition, 1969). The present description is based on information furnished by K. Yano, Kobe, Japan. (*See also* Ninuki-Renju.)

Halma

This game for four players on a chequered board of 16 x 16 squares was invented about 1880. Cheap boards are made of cardboard and the pieces are of wood or plastic; better quality boards are of veneered wood with light and dark squares. In the centre of each square is a drill-hole to receive the pegs of Halma' pieces made of bone or ivory.

Rules for Halma

1. Each player has thirteen pieces of his own colour arranged in his right hand corner of the board.

2. Only one piece may be moved in any turn of play.

3. When a player has finished a move the turn of play passes clockwise to the player on his left.

4. The pieces can move one square in any direction onto an empty adjacent square, or can jump by a short leap over a piece in any direction onto an empty square immediately beyond. A number of leaps may be made over his own or enemy pieces in a single turn of play, and players try to construct ladders to enable them to move their pieces several squares at a time. They may also make use of opponents' ladders, or attempt to block them to prevent their use by their owner.

5. The first player to occupy all the squares in the opposite corner to his own wins the game.

6. If there are only two players each has nineteen pieces which are placed in the player's right hand corner. The left hand corners are

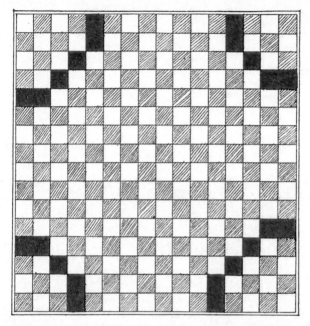

39. Halma board. Two of the corners are marked for 19 pieces used in the two-handed game. If there are four players each has 13 pieces.

left empty. All the other rules are the same as in the four-handed game.

The Conspirators

A board of 16 x 16 squares is used and the game is played on the points of intersection. A rectangle of 9 x 5 points is marked out in the middle of the board, and thirty-nine of the points on the periphery are designated as 'shelters'. The two players each have twenty pieces of their own colour.

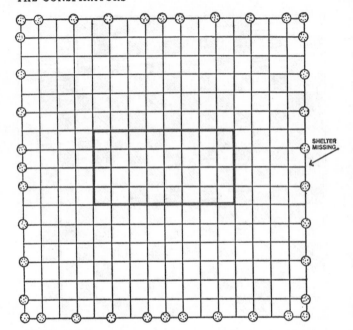

SHELTER MISSING

40. Empty board at the beginning of a game of The Conspirators. Note one 'Shelter' is missing, making 39 sanctuaries for the 40 conspirators.

Rules for The Conspirators

1. At the start of the game the board is empty and the pieces are placed one at a time by alternate turns of play on any of the forty-five points within the marked central rectangle. When all the pieces are placed the conspirators are meeting in secret.

2. With a warning that security forces are near, the conspirators attempt to hide. In turn each player moves one of his pieces one point in any direction: forwards, backwards, sideways or diagonally towards one of the thirty-nine shelters on the perimeter of the board.

3. Jumping over a piece of either colour by a short leap is allowed if there is a vacant point beyond, and multiple leaps in any direction can be made in the same turn of play.

4. The owner of the piece which fails to escape into a shelter loses the game.

Four players may take part, in which case each player has ten pieces of his own colour; otherwise the rules are the same as for the two-handed game.

(Translated from a French text by Miss Fiona Brookes.)

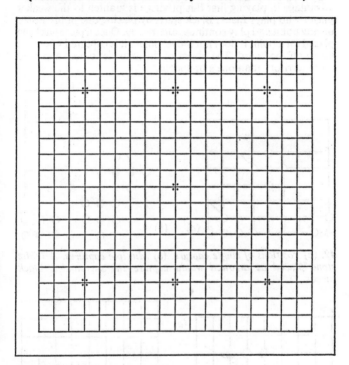

41. Board for I-go at the beginning of a game.

I-go or Go

Only a brief outline of this complicated game can be given here. Readers wishing to play Go should refer to the bibliography.

Go originated in China where it is known as Wei-ch'i, and was taken to Japan in the sixth century A.D. where it became fashionable in aristocratic circles. Its popularity spread throughout the country and now the quality and quantity of Japanese players greatly exceeds those in China.

The board consists of a grid of 361 intersections, nine of which are marked to assist in rapid orientation and in handicapping. Black has 181 black stones, and White 180 white stones. At the beginning of the game the board is empty and as there is a slight advantage in playing first this privilege is granted to the weaker player who plays Black. Black starts by placing one of his stones on any point and play continues alternately. Once a piece has been placed on a point it does not move, unless it is captured when it is taken off the board. The object of the game is to gain and hold more territory than one's opponent.

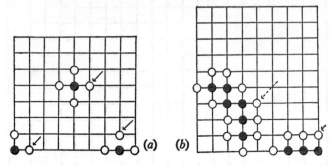

42. (a) Positions of single capture. (b) Multiple captures. A White stone placed as arrowed would capture the surrounded Black pieces.

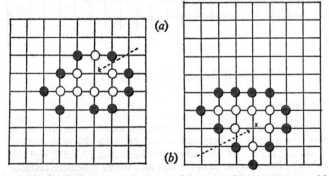

43. (a) Black cannot move on to the arrowed point as it would immediately be captured. (b) Black may move on to point x and thereby capture the seven White pieces.

Rules for I-go
1. Stones completely surrounded by opposing stones, and without any vacant points in orthogonal contact with them, are captured and removed from the board.
2. A stone cannot be placed on a point completely surrounded by enemy stones unless it makes a capture with the move; nor can a stone occupy the last free point of one of its own groups, unless it captures by this action.
3. Vacant points controlled by stones of one colour are called eyes, and as an eye can only be occupied by an opposing stone when it can make a capture, a group with two eyes is safe from attack.

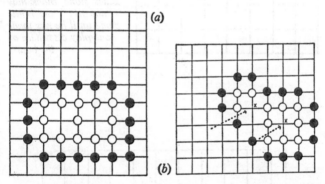

44. (*a*) *A safe White formation with two 'eyes'.* (*b*) *'False eyes'. Black may play on to the upper x point and capture three White pieces, and then two moves later play on to the lower x point and capture the remaining eight White pieces.*

4. A group of stones not in orthogonal contact may contain empty points, but the disconnected stones can be attacked, and the formation captured. Such false or temporary eyes are often constructed by a novice in error for real eyes.
5. A player may place a stone on any vacant point except to make an illegal play, or when his opponent has just captured a stone in a repetitive position known as a *ko*, when he must make one play elsewhere on the board, thus avoiding a perpetual position.
6. If there are three kos on the board the game is declared drawn.
7. Sometimes opposing formations of stones are interlocked in such a way that neither player can attack the other without losing his own pieces. This impasse is known as a *seki*, and these positions are left alone until the end of the game when they are neutralised

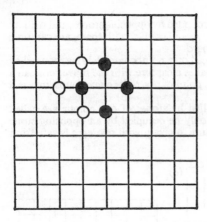

45. A repeating position or 'Ko'. If White plays on to the vacant point in the formation capturing one Black stone, Black may not attack the White stone until he has made one play elsewhere on the board.

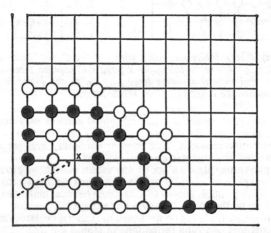

46. An impasse or 'seki'. Neither player can place a stone on x without losing his own formation. Expert players avoid 'seki' formations.

and all the free points within it are ignored and do not count to either player.

8. At the end of the game neutral vacant points between opposing formations which are valueless to both players are filled in with stones of either colour to help in adding up the final score.

9. Stones which inevitably can be surrounded are 'dead' and are removed at the end of the game without further play.

10. When the neutral points have been filled, and the dead stones removed from each player's territories, each player places the captured stones in his possession on vacant enemy points, thus reducing the opposing score by the number of pieces captured during the game.

11. The player with most vacant points held in his territories wins the game.

12. Equal players play Black alternately, but if one wins three times consecutively he usually gives his opponent a handicap of two stones, and if he continues to win the number is gradually increased until the weaker player wins a game.

Ninuki-Renju

This game is found throughout Japan though it is less popular than I-go or Gomoku-narabe, but like these games it has its experts who are graded into several ranks. Literally translated Ninuki-Renju means 'two (pieces) to take away to chain stones'.

Rules for Ninuki-Renju

1. The game is played on the I-go board with the same black and white stones (figure 41).

2. Black starts by placing a stone on any point on the board—White follows—and the players continue to place stones by alternate turns of play.

3. There are two methods of winning:
   a. By forming a complete contiguous chain of five stones on a column, row, or diagonal, as in Gomoku-narabe.
   b. By capturing ten of the opponent's pieces according to rule 4.

4. A player can remove from the board, and thus capture, any pair of opposing stones which are trapped between two of his own stones (figure 47).

5. A player is not permitted to place a stone on the board which will form two or more chains of three stones simultaneously; and

47. *Ninuki-Renju. The capture of two White stones trapped between two Black.*

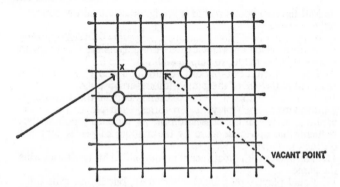

48. Ninuki-Renju. White is not allowed to place a stone on x which would contravene rule 5 in forming a 3-3 formation, although there is a vacant point in one of the limbs.

under this 3-3 chain rule is included a chain of three stones with a vacant point within itself (figure 48).

6. Forming a 3-3 chain formation is allowed, however, if it is the only way of preventing the opponent from forming a 4 or a 5 stone chain.

7. A chain of more than five stones is neutral and does not count towards victory or defeat.

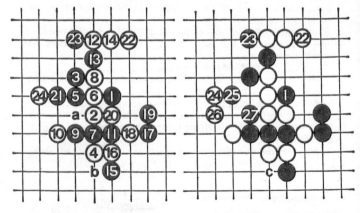

49. A game of Ninuki-Renju played in 1927 between the leading player at the time, K. Kubomatsu (white) and the present champion,

Y. Murashima, then a young man. Mr Kubomatsu's comments:

Black's 5: An interesting trial.

White's 10: Prevents Black coming on to this point.

White's 12 and 14: Ordinary, right moves.

Black 15: Right response.

White 16: if White comes, instead of 16, at first on to point 21, thus removing two Black pieces, then Black comes on to point 13. In this possible case, if White comes on to 16, Black responds with a. In the real play, however, White has come not on to 21, but to 16. If against this, White's 16, Black responds with a, then White comes on to 21—a 4-piece chain—and wins.

Black 17 and 19: Ordinary, right moves.

White 20: A provision for both the moves: (a) Black's a (capturing two White pieces) and (b) White's move on to 21 (capturing two Black pieces).

Black 27: After this move White gave up because he cannot prevent Black from moving on to c. But the too early move on to c, removing two White pieces, is wrong, for the following reason: if, against this move c, White's 22 and Black's 23 do not follow, Black cannot move on to 27, because it is a prohibited '3-3 move'.

The strategy around these moves has been quite exquisite and interesting. A refined good play.

Tablan

This game comes from south-west India and is still played in some of the villages in Mysore.

Rules for Tablan
1. The board consists of four rows of twelve squares and each player has twelve stones of his own colour. At the beginning of the game one stone stands on each square of the player's back row.
2. Four dicing sticks painted on one side and plain on the other are thrown up into the air, caught and thrown up again two or three times and then allowed to fall on the ground. The scoring is:
1 plain surface up—2 and throw again
4 plain surfaces up—8 and throw again
4 painted surfaces up—12 and throw again
No other throw scores and the sticks are passed to the opponent.
3. The first move of a piece can only be made on a throw of 2, though this throw can be split into two ones if required, and two pieces moved one square instead of one piece two squares.
4. Throws of 8 and 12 can be split into two fours and two sixes in the same way.

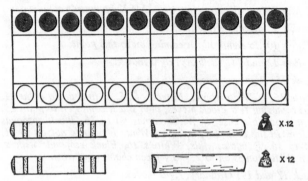

50. A Tablan board with the pieces in position for the beginning of a game. Below are four throwing sticks and one piece of each colour to show their shape.

5. The pieces move in the directions indicated in figure 51.
6. Pieces capture enemy pieces when they are on the two central rows, by landing on the same square, or when displacing them on the opponent's back row. Captured pieces are removed from the board.
7. Once a piece lands on a square on the opponent's back row it does not move again. It cannot be captured.
8. The enemy home row is captured, square by square, starting from a to l, (A to L).
9. More than one piece can be moved in any turn of play, and more than one capture can be made, but the pieces must move in the directions shown, and when they reach their last square on the middle rows they must turn off into the enemy home row and become immobilised. If they displace an enemy piece as they do so it is captured.

l	k	j	i	h	g	f	e	d	c	b	a
m	n	o	p	q	r	s	t	u	v	w	x
X	W	V	U	T	S	R	Q	P	O	N	M
A	B	C	D	E	F	G	H	I	J	K	L

51. A diagram to show the direction of movement of the White pieces. The Black pieces move in the same direction.

10. There is no doubling up of pieces.

11. A player must use a throw, convenient or not, unless he has only one piece left near the end of the middle row next to the enemy back row, and the throw does not allow him to occupy a square. These squares must be occupied one after another in order (*see* rule 8).

12. The player capturing most enemy squares is the winner.

4. MANCALA GAMES

Pallanguli

Pallanguli is popular in southern India among the Tamil and is one of a large family of similar games known as the Mancala group. This series of games is named after Mankala'h, a game which was widely played in the coffee shops in Egypt in the early nineteenth century when it became known to the western world.

The board consists of a thick plank of wood with two rows of seven holes, and a large store at either end. The players sit facing each other across the board, having placed six seeds in each of his holes, and leaving his store empty (figure 52).

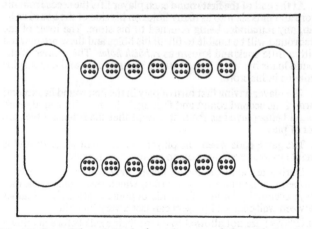

52. A Pallanguli board. Each player has seven holes with six stones in each, and a store hole.

Rules for Pallanguli

1. The game continues by alternate turns of play.

2. The opening player lifts the seeds from any hole on his side of the board, leaving it empty, and passing in an anti-clockwise direction sows one seed into each contiguous hole. If he reaches the end of his side of the board he sows in his opponent's holes, still in the same direction. When the last seed of a lift falls into a hole, either on his own side of the board, or his opponent's, he picks up all the pieces in the next hole and continues sowing as before in the same direction.

3. If the last seed of a lift falls into a hole with an empty hole beyond, any seeds in the hole immediately beyond the empty hole are captured and put into the player's store. He then continues play from the next loaded hole, but if the last seed of a lift falls into a hole with two empty holes beyond he wins nothing and his turn ceases.

4. His opponent then lifts the seed or seeds from any hole on his side of the board and sows in an anti-clockwise direction. His turn also ceases when the last seed falls into a hole with two empty holes immediately beyond.

5. Four seeds in a hole are called a *cow* and, irrespective of the sower, become the property of the owner of the hole and are lifted at once and placed in his store while play continues.

6. At the end of the first round each player lifts the seeds from his store and puts six into as many holes on his side of the board as he can, any remainder being returned to his store. The loser of the first round will be unable to fill all his holes and these are marked with a little stick and known as *rubbish holes*. The winner of the round loads his seven holes with six seeds in each and any surplus remains in his store.

7. The player having first turn of play in the first round has second turn in the second round and first again in the third round, each round being played as the first, except that the rubbish holes are out of play.

8. The game ends when one player has less than six seeds and is unable to load even one hole to begin a new round.

9. During a round the losing player may win enough seeds to re-open one or more rubbish holes, which then come back into play; eventually he may force his opponent into defeat. Games between well-matched players can last a very long time.

10. Players are not allowed to count their seeds before making a lift, but a skilled player can decide at a glance the best lifts on the board.

Gabata

Until the publication of a most important article by Richard Pankhurst in the *Ethiopia Observer* (Vol XIV, No 3, 1971) Three Rank Mancala was thought to be obsolete. Pankhurst records, however, that several varieties are still played in Ethiopia and neighbouring countries one of which, Gabata, is described below.

Gabata is played in the central highlands of Eritrea on a board of three rows of six holes each. Half the holes belong to player P, (A to I), and the rest to player p, (a to i), as shown in figure 53.

p

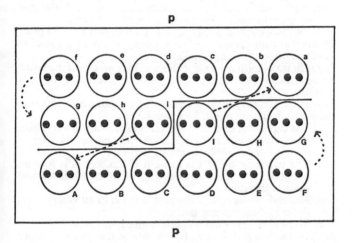

P

53. A diagram of a board for Gabata, showing three stones in each hole; and the direction of play.

Method of play

1. The game begins with three pebbles in each hole, and the players start simultaneously by lifting the entire contents of their left-hand hole in their back row (P begins at hole A—p at hole a) and sowing one pebble into the adjacent holes in an anti-clockwise direction. On sowing the last pebble into any hole the player lifts the entire contents of the hole, including the pebble he has just dropped into it. and continues to sow them in the same direction into the adjacent holes. P thus starts from hole A and sows along his back row from left to right, along his half of the middle row from right to left, and then passes to the opponent's back row

travelling from right to left (hole a to hole f) and then along his opponent's half of the middle row from left to right (hole g to hole i). He then passes to his own back row at hole A and continues as before, until one of the players finishes a lift at an empty hole.

Up to this point the game is merely a race between the players. The first player to come to a halt begins the second phase of the game when the players alternate their turns of play according to the following rules:

2. Each player always starts from one of his own holes by picking up its entire contents and he sows them one at a time into the contiguous holes following the specified direction of play.

3. If the last pebble of a lift falls into an occupied hole, he picks up its entire contents and continues sowing until he finally finishes sowing a lift into an empty hole.

4. On finishing a lift in an empty hole on his own side of the board he captures any pebbles in an enemy hole or holes along the same column.

5. He then lifts the pebble which made the capture and sows it in the next hole, giving rise to four possibilities:

    a. The capture of further pebbles from the enemy if the pebble falls into one of the player's holes which is empty, facing an occupied hole or holes in enemy territory.

    b. The continuation of the move if the pebble falls into an occupied hole, the entire contents of which are lifted and sown in the usual way.

    c. The end of the turn if the pebble lands in an empty hole, faced by empty enemy holes.

    d. The end of the turn if it falls into an empty enemy hole.

6. Play continues until one player's side of the board is empty His opponent then lifts all the remaining pebbles and adds them to his previous winnings.

7. The two players then load their holes again, three pebbles in each, in an anti-clockwise direction starting at the hole in their left-hand corner.

8. If the two players have captured different numbers of pebbles the weaker player fills as many holes as he can, being allowed to fill the last hole with two, or even one pebble instead of the usual three. His opponent fills the corresponding hole on his side of the board with the same number of pebbles, and places the remainder aside as his winnings. Part of the board is thus left empty, but the holes in the vacant area continue to belong to their original owners and are played over in the same way as in the opening round.

Eventually one player will capture all the pebbles, and his opponent will concede defeat.

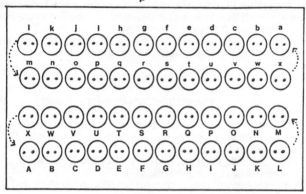

54. A diagram of a Baré board, each hole containing two pebbles. The arrows show the direction of movement. Each player only uses the holes on his own side of the board.

Baré

Baré is played by the Anuak people of Ethiopia's far-west, on a board of four rows of twelve holes with two pebbles in each hole. The players own the two rows nearest to them and only move in these rows, capturing pebbles from the opposing two rows.

Rules for Baré
1. The players start simultaneously from any hole in either of their rows by picking up the two pebbles in the hole and sowing them in the contiguous holes in an anti-clockwise direction, picking up the entire contents of the hole in which the last pebble fell and continuing in this way until the last pebble of a lift falls into an empty hole. At this moment the first phase of the game ends.
2. The player who first reaches an empty hole begins the next stage of the game by lifting all the pebbles from any hole in his front or rear row, providing that it contains two or more pebbles, and sowing them one by one into the ensuing holes. He picks up the contents of the hole in which the last pebble fell, and stops when the last pebble in his hand falls into an empty hole.
3. The players have alternate turns of play.
4. Captures are made by a player sowing the last pebble in his hand into a hole in his front row which contains one or more

pebbles, while the two opposite enemy holes are both occupied. The player then lifts the pebbles from these enemy holes and sows them one at a time into his own holes starting immediately beyond the one from which he made the capture.

5. On the completion of this manoeuvre the player continues his turn of play by picking up and sowing pebbles from any of his holes.

6. If a player fails to lift enemy pebbles he could have captured, his opponent may amalgamate these pebbles into one of the two holes concerned, thus protecting them from further attack for the rest of the turn.

7. If a player forgets to amalgamate pebbles in one hole under rule 6, and subsequently his opponent attacks them again, they are captured in the usual way.

8. The game ends when one player has only singletons left in his holes when he can no longer make a lift.

Tactics: each player tries to keep his pebbles on his right, and to capture those opposite him on his left.

This form of mancala is unusual in that a game finishes with a single setting of the board.

---

5. CALCULATION GAMES

Rithmomachia

At least three manuscripts of the eleventh century, two of the twelfth and one each of the thirteenth and fourteenth centuries survive, describing this medieval game which may have originated at Byzantium or Alexandria, and was based on the Pythagorean philosophy of numbers. The first mention of the game was by Hermannus Contractus (A.D. 1013-1054).

Rithmomachia was played on a board of 8 x 16 plain squares, and the pieces were in the shapes of rounds, triangles, squares and pyramids. The pieces of one side were white and the other black, being known respectively as the Evens and the Odds. Dots below the numbers served to distinguish 6 from 9, 18 from 81, et cetera.

The pieces were arranged for play as in figure 55 which is taken from de Boussiere's work of 1554. The players moved their pieces alternately, a round moving onto any adjacent empty space, a triangle moving three empty spaces in any direction and a square four spaces in any direction. The pyramid could move like any of the layers of which it was composed. No piece could leap over any other piece, and the L-shaped movement of the Knight in chess was not permitted. The players sat facing the longer sides of

WHITE   ODD

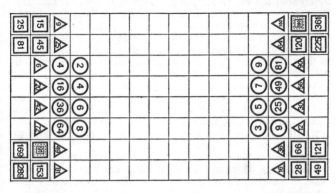

EVEN   BLACK

55. A Rithmomachia board with the pieces arranged at the beginning of a game.

the board although the pieces were arranged along the shorter rows.

The object of the game was to capture the opponent's pieces to form some desired combination.

Methods of capture
1. By Meeting: if Even's Triangle 25, by advancing three spaces, could land on Odd's Round 25, Even would not move his piece, but would take up his opponent's.
2. By Assault: if a smaller number, multiplied by the number of vacant spaces between it and the larger one, equalled the larger one, it could take it. For example, Odd's Round 5 could take Even's Square 45 if nine spaces separated them.
3. By Ambuscade: if two pieces whose sum equalled the number on an opponent's piece could be moved onto the spaces on either side of it, the latter was ambuscaded and removed. For example, if Even's Rounds 4 and 8 could move on either side of Odd's Triangle 12, the latter was removed from the board.
4. By Siege: if a piece was surrounded on all four sides by enemy pieces, it was captured and removed.

Pyramids, of which there was one on each side, were constructed of a pile of the different types of pieces. Even's pyramid of 91 was built up of two squares (36 and 25), two triangles (16 and 9) and two rounds (4 and 1). Odd's pyramid of 190 was built of two squares (64 and 49), two triangles (36 and 25) and one round (16). Pyramids were rarely captured except by siege. They were therefore subject to a special attack and were considered to be threatened whenever one of its constituent layers was attacked by any of the four methods. A ransom, however, was permitted; a piece of the same value as the layer attacked being offered instead. If no such piece was available, due to previous capture, any other piece could be given that the opponent was willing to accept.

As the pyramids could not be captured if the numbers 91 and 190 were retained, capture was permitted if the base square was successfully attacked, namely 36 (Even's), or 64 (Odd's). The pyramids had no special value, but these different methods of attack made play more interesting.

The object of the game was to capture the opponent's pieces to gain a Victory, which was possible in eight different ways. Before beginning a game the players agreed on the type of Victory they intended to achieve. Five of the Victories were known as Common Victories which were suitable for beginners, and the other three as Proper Victories which were the aim of skilled players.

The Common Victories were:

1. *De corpore:* the players agreed in advance upon some number as the target. If this were twenty for instance, as soon as either player captured twenty of the opponent's pieces he won the game.

2. *De bonis:* this depended upon the value of the captured pieces. Perhaps 160 was agreed upon as the winning number, and as soon as one player held opposing pieces whose sum was 160 or more he had won the game.

3. *De lite:* this depended upon the value of the pieces and the number of digits inscribed on them. If 160 were chosen there would be a further condition that the total number of digits on the pieces should equal some small number such as eight. A player would then try to capture pieces like 56, 64, 28 and 15, equalling eight digits; but not 121, 9 and 30 equalling six digits.

4. *De honore:* this depended upon the number of the pieces and their value. Again taking 160 as the agreed number for the sum of the values, some other number like five would be chosen for the number of pieces, when 56, 64, 28 and 12 or 121, 9, and 30 would not bring Victory while 64, 36, 30, 25 and 5 would, as it fulfilled the two conditions.

5. *De honore liteque:* the players might agree upon 160 for the value, five for the number of pieces, and nine for the number of digits. Odd could win with the capture of 64, 36, 42, 16 and 2; or Even with 64, 36, 30, 25 and 5.

The Proper Victories used by expert players resulted from combinations related to arithmetic, geometric and harmonic progressions. In each of these Victories the pieces, one of which must be an opponent's, were displayed in the selected progression on the opponent's side of the board.

6. *Victoria Magna:* this consisted of an arrangement of three counters in any one of the three simple progressions. There are forty-one possible combinations with an arithmetic progression, eighteen in geometric progression, and seventeen in harmonic progression. The possibilities are greater for Even in the arithmetic, for Odd in the geometric, and equal in the harmonic. One of these arrangements, in harmonic progression, is 6, 8, 12.

7. *Victoria Major* consisted of a combination of two out of three progressions: arithmetic and geometric; geometric and harmonic; or harmonic and arithmetic. This Victory was obtained by bringing four pieces in line in the enemy's territory, two of which had to belong to one of the selected progressions, and two to the other. For example, 2,3,4,8, would gain a Victoria Major for either Even or Odd; for 2,3,4, are in arithmetic progression, and 2,4,8, are in geometric; where 2,4,8, are Even's pieces, and 3 is Odd's piece. There are sixty-one such double progressions, all of which are available to Odd, and all but one to Even.

8. *Victoria Excellentissima:* this was the most difficult of all the Victories and represented the pinnacle of the game, requiring four numbers in a row which embodied all three progressions. There are only six possible solutions: (2,3,4,6,); (4,6,8,12,); (7,8,9,12,); (4,6,9,12,); (3,5,15,25,); and (12,15,16,20,).

Outstanding intellectuals of the Middle Ages became addicted to Rithmomachia and regarded the game as superior to chess. Today it is completely forgotten and is unlikely to enjoy a revival for there is now no interest in the number theory upon which it was based. However, mathematicians may care to consider the principles of its construction which are explained in the appendix below.

Mathematical appendix to Rithmomachia

In figure 56 the round pieces in the fourth row on each side consisted of odd and even numbers respectively. The round pieces on the third row were the squares of the fourth row pieces and the sum of the pieces in these two rows gave the value of the triangles on the second row immediately behind them. The triangles at the sides of the third row were formed from the triangles on row two by means of a relation known as *super particularis*—the number is found by joining the corresponding number in the second row to an aliquot part of it, determined by the number in the round in the fourth row. For example, 81 is obtained from 72 by adding $\frac{1}{8}$ of 72, 8 being the number in the

56. *A diagram to show the derivation of the numbers in Rithmomachia.*

round on the fourth row of that column. Similarly $49 = 42 + \frac{1}{6}$ of 42: $25 = 20 + \frac{1}{4}$ of 20: $9 = 6 + \frac{1}{2}$ of 6.

The squares on the second row were formed by adding the respective triangles, $9 + 6 = 15$: $25 + 20 = 45$. But one square on each side, 91 for the Evens and 190 for the Odds, is replaced by a pyramid. These pyramids were formed by placing squares of decreasing size on top of each other, and demonstrated the construction of the numbers they carried. Thus $91 = 6^2 + 5^2 + 4^2 + 3^2 + 2^2 + 1^2$; and $190 = 8^2 + 7^2 + 6^2 + 5^2 + 4^2$.

The Even pyramid (91) containing the squares of all numbers from 1 to 6 was called a perfect pyramid, but the Odd pyramid (190) which lacked $3^2 + 2^2 + 1^2$ was known as *tricurta* (thrice curtailed).

The squares on the first row were obtained from the rounds in the fourth row by the following formula: if the number in the round on the fourth row was n, and the number on the square on the second row was s, the number on the square in the first row was given by the formula

$$\left(\frac{2n + 1}{n + 1}\right)s$$

thus $\left(\frac{2 \times 2 + 1}{2 + 1}\right) \times 15 = \frac{5}{3} \times 15 = 25$

or $\left(\frac{2 \times 4 + 1}{4 + 1}\right) \times 45 = \frac{9}{5} \times 45 = 81$ etc.

6. DICE GAMES

Shut the Box

Although elaborate boards have been used for this game for any number of players the basic equipment is satisfied by a piece of paper, nine coins and two cubic dice. A square containing nine boxes is drawn on the paper and numbered from 1 to 9. The players in turn attempt to shut the boxes.

Rules for Shut the Box

1. The player in play throws the two dice, and then uses the score to cover the numbers (close the boxes) on the board. With a throw of 6:3: he can use the aggregate and place a coin to conceal the 9, or use each score separately and place a coin on 6 and 3.

2. He then throws again and once more has the choice of using the aggregate if this is possible, or one or both individual scores on the dice to close boxes.

3. If he is unable to close at least one box on a throw his turn ceases, and the sum of the numbers remaining exposed is counted against him. The board is cleared and the dice are passed to the next player.

4. When a player has accumulated forty-five or more points he drops out of the game.

5. If the aggregate of the numbers left exposed on the board is six or less, one die is discarded. Throws continue with the other die until all the boxes are shut, or the player is confronted with a score which he cannot use, when his turn ceases.

6. The last player left in the game is the winner.

(The author is indebted to Mr John Mosesson for a description of this game.)

57. Board for Shut the Box.

Four Numbers

Four Numbers is a Chinese gambling game using a four-sided top and a Fan Tan board. The top is marked 1:2:3:4: on its four faces, and is spun in a saucer and covered with a cup or bowl while still spinning. When all the stakes have been placed on the board the cover of the saucer is raised exposing the winning number uppermost which is called out. Winning players retain their stakes and are paid their dividends by the banker, while the losing stakes are gathered from the board and passed to him. Players then place their bets for the next round.

Method of placing bets

1. *Koo Fan:* the stake is placed in the centre of the First House. If 'one' is called as winner, the player is paid three times his stake. The stake is lost if 'two', 'three', or 'four' is called.

2. *Kok:* the stake is placed on the dividing line between the First and Second Houses. If 'one' or 'two' is called as winner the player is paid a dividend equal to his stake. The stake is lost if 'three' or 'four' is called.

3. *Lim:* the stake is placed in the First House adjacent to the Second House. If 'one' is called as winner, the player receives twice his stake; if 'two' is called his stake is returned to him, and it is lost with a call of 'three' or 'four'.

4. *Chuen:* the stake is placed in the First House on the line separating it from the empty central square. If 'one' or 'three' is called, a dividend equal to the stake is paid to the player. The stake is lost with a call of 'two' or 'four'.

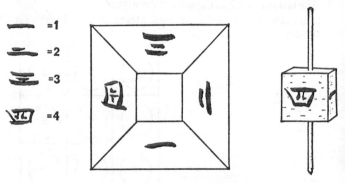

58. Board and teetotum used for the Chinese game of Four Numbers.

5. *Tong:* the stake is placed in the First House adjacent to the vacant central square. If 'one' is called, the player receives twice his stake; the stake is returned to him if 'three' is called, and is lost if the call is 'two' or 'four'.

6. *Cheng Tau:* the stake is placed outside the First House near the base line. If 'one' is called a dividend equal to the stake is paid to the player; if 'two' or 'four' is called his stake is returned to him; and if 'three' is called the stake is lost.

These six methods of laying stakes in House One apply to stakes laid in any of the other houses. The odds are fair, and to pay for overheads and make a profit the management deducts 10 per cent from every winning dividend.

Top and Five Balls

This game is an old favourite of villagers in the Dolomites for passing the time on winter evenings. The bowl, pockets, top and balls are made of beechwood, the pockets being glued to the sides of the bowl. The top has a six-sided base, the sides being unequal, thus increasing the element of luck.

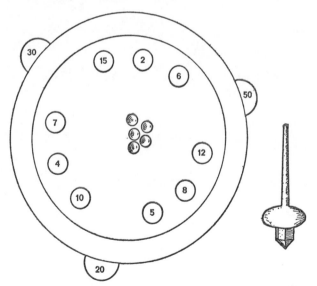

59. Board, top, and five wooden balls used in Top and Five Balls.

75

Rules for Top and Five Balls

1. Before each player's turn the five wooden balls, four of plain wood and one painted red, are placed in the centre of the bowl. The player then spins the top using a sliding movement of the palms with the stem of the top between them.

2. When the top stops spinning the score is added up, any score by the red ball being tripled.

3. If a ball jumps out of the bowl it is replaced as long as the top is still spinning and there is a chance of it making a score.

4. The players play to an agreed total, commonly 301.

5. Any number of players may take part.

Although the way the balls strike the top is pure luck, skill in spinning the top will produce higher scores during the course of an evening's play.

MAKING BOARDS AND PIECES

Satisfactory equipment for all the games described in this book can be made at home without difficulty. The designs should be drawn on Bristol board or thin card with Indian ink and a ruler, and the finished drawing covered with a sheet of perspex or glass, or varnished. Many Georgian and Victorian race games were printed on thin paper, mounted in sections on a linen backing similar to modern better quality road-maps. Readers may like to try drawing on paper, hand-colouring with crayon or paint, and then sectioning the design into rectangles and pasting them with thin glue onto a sheet of linen. Protective covers are made from cardboard.

A wide variety of objects will serve as pieces: coloured stones, acorns, marbles, nuts, pop-tops, buttons and corks—all are readily available—though craftsmen and do-it-yourself enthusiasts may like to express their ingenuity and skill. Attractive Dablot Prejjesne sets were made by Lapplanders using only a knife to whittle branches of fir. A lathe is not essential in making gaming pieces although it can be very helpful and certainly speeds production.

Dice of various shapes, throwing sticks and teetotums, are also all well within the capability of anyone accustomed to using their hands.

BIBLIOGRAPHY

Readers requiring more information about the games in this book will find many of them described in greater detail in *Board and Table Games of Many Civilizations* by the author (Volumes I and II; O.U.P., 1960 and 1970 respectively). The following works have been selected for their clarity and availability.

Chess in Iceland; W. Fiske; Florence, 1905.

Table Games of Georgian and Victorian Days; F. B. R. White-house; P. Garnet; London, 1951.

Ur, the First Phase; Sir Leonard Woolley; London, 1946.

History of Chess; H. J. R. Murray; O.U.P., 1913. (Burmese, Siamese and Chinese chess.)

Sho-gi, Japan's Game of Strategy; T. Leggett; Rutland, Vermont, 1966. (Japanese chess.)

Go Games for Beginners; H. Kambayashi; Japan Publications Trading Co., 1964.

How to Play Go; K. Takagawa; printed in Japan, 1956.

The Vital Points of Go; K. Takagawa; printed in Japan, 1958.

INDEX

Achi, 49, fig. 36
Alquerque 32–33, 36, fig. 21
Amerindian games, 14
Arab games, 33
Archaeological importance of games, 3–4, 6, 8
Ashta-pada, 21
Backgammon, 10–11, 12, 35, fig. 6
Baré, 67–68, fig. 54
Barrikade, 21
Burmese Chess, 24–26, figs. 12, 13
Carter, H., 6
Chasing the Girls, 11–12, fig. 7
Chess, 35:
    Burmese, 24–26, figs. 12, 13
    Chinese, 26–27, fig. 15
    Farmers', see Gala
    Gala, 29–31, figs. 17, 18
    Japanese, see Sho-gi
    Shaturanga, 21–24, fig. 11
    Sho-gi, 27–29, fig. 16
    Siamese, 26, fig. 14
Chinese Chess, 26–27, fig. 15
Chinese games, 26, 48, 74
Conspirators, 53–55, fig. 40
Dablot Prejjesne, 42–45, 76, figs. 31, 32
Dice:
    Cubic, 8, 11, 16, 19, 73, fig. 4
    Long, 22, fig. 11
    Pyramidal, 6, fig. 2
Dolomites, 75
Draughts, 35–36, 37, 39, fig. 23:
    Continental, 29, 36–37, fig. 24
Draughtsboard, 37, 39, figs. 23, 24, 26
Egypt, 3, 4, 50
Egyptian games, 3–4, 6, 50, 63
Ethiopia Observer, 65
Ethiopian games, 65–66, 67–68
Faience, 3, 7
Fanorona, 34–35, fig. 22
Fan Tan board, fig. 58
Farmers' Chess, see Gala
Four Field Kono, 31, fig. 19

Four Numbers, 74–75, fig. 58
Fox and Geese, 40–41, fig. 28
Gabata, 65–66, fig. 53
Gala, 29–31, figs. 17, 18
Generals' Game, The, see Sho-gi
Georgian and Victorian race games, 16–19, 76
German games, 29–31
Go, 55–59, figs. 41–46: board, 37, 39, 51, 59
Gomoku-narabe, 51–52, fig. 38
Hala-tafl, see Fox and Geese
Halma, 52–53, fig. 39
Hong Kong, 27
Icelandic games, 11–12, 40–41
I-go, see Go
Indian games, 14–16, 21–24, 39–40, 61–63, 63–64
Japanese games, 27–29, 51–52, 55–59, 59–61
Javanese games, 32–33
Jubilee, The, 18–19
Korean games, 12–14, 31
Lambs and Tigers, 39–40, fig. 27
Lapland games, 41, 42
Ludo, 16
Ludus Duodecim Scriptorum, 8, fig. 4
Madagascar, 34
Maori games, 48, fig. 35
Meijin-sen, 29
Ming Mang, 37–39, figs. 25, 26
Mu Torere, 48–49, fig. 48
Mysore, 60
Negro games, 49
Nine Men's Morris, 50–51, fig. 37
Ninuki-Renju, 59–61, figs. 47–49
Norse games, 40–41, 41–42, 42–45, 50
Nyout, 12–14, fig. 8
Pachisi, 14–16, fig. 9
Pallanguli, 63–64, fig. 52
Palm Tree game, 4
Pasang, 19–21, fig. 10.
Pong hau k'i, 48, fig. 34
Pulijudam, see Lambs and Tigers

79

Pythagoras, 3, 68
Quirkat, *see* Alquerque
Renju, 51–52, fig. 38
Reversi, 37
Ringo, 46–47, fig. 33
Rithmomachia, 68–72, figs. 55, 56
Roman games, 8
Royal Geographical Amusement, 17–18
Royal Tombs of Ur, 6, 12
Senat, 3, 6–7
Shatranj, 24
Shaturanga, 21–24, fig. 11
Shell, 6, 15
Sho-gi, 27–29, fig. 16
Shut the Box, 73, fig. 57
Siamese Chess, 26, fig. 14
Sticks, gambling, 7, 13, figs. 3, 8
Surakarta, 32–33, fig. 20

Tablan, 62–63, fig. 50
Tabula, 8–10, fig. 5
Tablut, 41–42, figs. 29–30
Tee-totum, 17
Thirty Squares, game of, 3, 6–7, fig. 3
Three Rank Mancala, 65
Tibetan games, 37–39
Top and Five Balls, 75–76, fig. 59
Tric-trac, 10–11, fig. 6
Tutankhamun, King, 6:
London exhibition, 7
Ur, 6, 12
Wei-ch'i, 55–59, figs. 41–46
Wessex culture, 3
Whitehouse, F.R.B., 17
Woolley, Sir Leonard, 6
Zohn Ahl, 14